Encountering
GOD
in the Stillness

THE NORTH SHORE STORY

T. Alan Stumbo

WESTBOW
PRESS
A DIVISION OF THOMAS NELSON

Scripture taken from the Holy Bible, New International Version®. Copyright ©
1973, 1978, 1984 Biblica. Used by permission of Zondervan. All rights reserved.

WestBow Press books may be ordered through booksellers or by contacting:

WestBow Press
A Division of Thomas Nelson
1663 Liberty Drive
Bloomington, IN 47403
www.westbowpress.com
1-(866) 928-1240

ISBN: 978-1-4497-3604-0 (sc)
ISBN: 978-1-4497-3605-7 (hc)
ISBN: 978-1-4497-3603-3 (e)

Library of Congress Control Number: 2011963679

Printed in the United States of America

WestBow Press rev. date: 01/16/2012

"Our familiarity with the text, "In quietness and confidence shall be your strength (Isaiah 30:15)," does not often translate into practical and, at the simultaneously, very spiritual reality. While we acknowledge the meaningfulness of God's statement, we give it a passing nod and continue right on in our fast-moving lives without making any significant changes. T. Alan Stumbo's beautiful illustration of God's formula for spiritual strength could and should be used of the Lord to bring an alteration to your life style. Read it for personal enjoyment, but more than that, for personal improvement. If you allow the Lord to accomplish His purposes in you through the enjoyable hours you spend with this book, those hours will bear eternal fruit."

----**Dr. Charles W. Shepson**

Contents

Dedication

To my loving wife, Rachelle, thank you for seeing something about me worth waiting for. My goodness, what a patient and enduring soul you are. Thank you for prodding me along, each step of the way. You are a tremendous tool in the hand of God, and a faithful partner on the journey of life. I pray that your rewards will be great.

Introduction

"For I know the plans I have for you," declares the LORD,
"plans to prosper you and not to harm you, plans to give you
hope and a future."
~Jeremiah 29:11

W hen I was a young boy, I loved to read history books. I loved adventurous tales of men and women who would leave behind the comforts of society in search of remote territories to settle and call their own. Then, there were the mountain men, the trappers, and the explorers, who form the legends that young boys dream about. In my little fantasy world, I would ride the rapids with Lewis and Clark. I would blaze the trails with Daniel Boone. On long winter nights, I would sit by the fire with Laura, and the rest of the Ingalls Family, as we listened intently to the boyhood tales that Charles would recollect. There was something about their lives that we will rarely experience in our push-button society. They seemed to have discovered the secret of contentment, while never really having any material abundance of their own to speak of.

I will admit that I enjoy a lot of the modern conveniences we have, but there is also a part of me that has always yearned for a simpler, more rustic way of life. I guess I was about eight years old the first time I realized how much I loved the simple beauty that I could find in nature. I was fascinated with most outdoor shows, but I was especially drawn to those that centered on the lakes and forests of the Northern Hemisphere. I used to daydream of riding a train to some wild part of Alaska to homestead some undisturbed lakeside expanse. It would be a section of land like the ones I had seen in my real estate catalog that I ordered from the back section of a fishing magazine.

Then, during one special summer, I had my first wilderness experience. My father took my two nephews and me on a weeklong fishing trip to the Boundary Waters Canoe Area near the town of Ely, Minnesota. I immediately fell in love with the tall pines lining the rocky shorelines. I had never seen such crystal clear water in any of our lakes back home in Iowa. We caught fish from the lake, that until then, we had only dreamed about as we perused fishing magazines. We enjoyed the simple tasks, like cutting our daily supply of wood, cooking our meals over an open fire, and washing our dishes in the lake. We spent the nights drinking all of my dad's coffee, and lying on our backs staring up at the vast constellations of stars, which were beautifully visible with no smog of civilization to hinder the view. I have never forgotten that fishing trip, and since then I have never felt at home in the bustling, crowded city. In the past, it seemed like every time my nephews and I would spend some time together, we were always dreaming about a future day when we could find a way to escape the confines of the city, and return to the unspoiled beauty we had shared on that little island as young boys.

These days, we just sit around and talk about politics, church, sports, our wives, our jobs, and we realize that civilization has bound us with chords of duty and routine. There is no way we can make those old dreams become a reality without greatly affecting someone within our sphere of influence, whether it be our wives, our kids, or the careers that conspire with civilization to keep us corralled behind imaginary fences. I still dream of that little homestead nestled in the corner of some northern meadow, but the dream has become a little fuzzy now when I stroll around its boundaries.

Sometimes, the closest we come to our dreams, is by helping others achieve theirs. That is what I was doing when I joined my brother with the ambition of restoring a neglected, old resort. I wasn't sure whether I was being teased with envy while building a dream that belonged to someone else, or if it could have been divine whispers encouraging me not to let the residue of my own dreams slip away. It is a good feeling when those dormant desires begin to rise up once again. It is like coming home after a long journey, yet finding that you had never left.

I remember catching a glimpse of my forgotten dream the first day I drove on to the resort property. The windows of my car were rolled down and the warm, aromatic smell of sun-baked pine needles greeted me. It was as comforting as stumbling into the kitchen on a blustery winter day to the sight and smell of your mother's fresh, baked cinnamon rolls cooling on the counter. In addition to the smell of pine needles, the crashing waves on the rocky shoreline misted the air with another old, familiar smell that spirited me back across the decades before there were bills, wedding bells, and time clocks. My memories returned to that carefree day long ago, when my nephews and I cheered with excitement as waves splashed over the hull while we sped to our secluded island in the wilderness.

What had once seemed like the only option to a fruitless job search had quickly become a blessed return to the simpler foundations of my life that I had wandered away from, and with the passing of time, almost forgotten. It is peculiar how the work of our hands can mirror the stage of life we are going through in the present. Here I had come to restore neglected, old buildings, and found that I was experiencing an inner restoration of my own. It was good to smell the sawdust from newly cut cedar boards. The scent spoke to me of new beginnings, or was it really a return to something that desperately needed to be unearthed and brought to life again?

At times, it had seemed like the project would never be completed. There are some steps involved in renovation work that must be carried out patiently, and delicately, in order to preserve the valuable handiwork of the original craftsman. It was the renovation work at the heart of the building structure that took the most time, as we stripped away damaged or unnecessary edifices that would detract from the beauty and strength of the new structure. The new construction progressed rather quickly once all of the demolition and restoration work was completed. After a few months the tired, old cabin began to slowly change, and piece-by-piece the true beauty of the project began to unfold.

The total time required to repair and renovate the main cabin took over two years, but it seemed to take much longer. It was during this time of solitude and contemplation that I began to notice the inner transformation that God was working out inside me. We expect a renovation project like the old cabin to involve a lot of time, sweat, and sacrifice. Nevertheless, are we not mistaken to somehow believe that our own transformation should be any less time-consuming and difficult? We lose heart when our path becomes too steep, and the hopes of once-passionate ambitions slowly slip away as we write them off as being either too lofty, or impractical. Despite what our common sense, and experience tells us, is it not possible that it could have been the creative breath of God that conceived our now fallow dreams in the first place, no matter how raw and imperfect they may have seemed at one time? I am becoming a firm believer that nothing of great value is discovered quickly. Haste only diminishes the intensity of the heartfelt joy experienced when dreams do come true at last. We should never give up on our God-given dreams. We should simply look to God patiently as He reveals what facets of our dreams represent His true vision for our lives. If those early dreams have been reduced to smoldering coals, we should ask God to breathe life into them again until they are rekindled, and set ablaze once more.

Our Heavenly Father is always speaking to us, however soft that voice may seem. He is always coaxing and wooing us, challenging and transforming us, and all the while planting in our hearts the seeds of a better dream that will one day blossom into something far better than we could ever have imagined in our own creativity. When those better dreams become fully alive they will be in sync with the plans and purposes God has always envisioned for our lives.

From the first glance, this book may appear to be just another story, but in reality it goes much deeper than "just a story." You will see how the project took on new meaning as God began to reveal to me the way He sometimes speaks into our lives through even the most insignificant things we take for granted. This book is a call to believers from all walks of life to slow down, and listen for God's voice. Not with the physical ears, but through total awareness and expectancy that God has something to say to us in every single way we perceive our circumstances and surroundings. We can learn to tie together our experiences in much the same way that a person would look at the pieces of a puzzle to find out where a particular piece fits in the bigger picture. This book will challenge you to throw off every hindrance, or distraction that is impeding a deeper relationship with God. It is an illustration of how work; any work, can become a form of worship when the Spirit of God is welcomed to join the task at hand. It expresses the joy of hearing the still, small voice of God after it has not been heard for a long season, or if it has been discovered for the very first time. Once you hear His voice, the insignificant becomes extraordinary, and what appears to be just a wilderness will become for you a door of hope opening to an oasis of life-giving renewal.

<u>Chapter One</u>

~The Gift of Solitude~

"Therefore I am now going to allure her; I will lead her into the wilderness and speak tenderly to her. There I will give her back her vineyards, and will make the Valley of Achor a door of hope..."
~ Hosea 2:14,15

I could feel it in my spirit; something really special was going to take place. What it was, I was not sure, but after following the Lord for quite some time, I could tell this "thing" had His fingerprints all over it. If you ever spend very much time in the Psalms, or Lamentations, you will soon see that God does not take pleasure in, nor does He waste any of our suffering. He is a loving Father that tests and teaches His children, but always for our ultimate benefit.

There is a purpose for the trials and struggles we face in this life. In fact, the Lord Jesus said we are to expect them as His followers. If He, being the Son of God, had to suffer in the body, then we can expect to experience suffering because of our association with Him. There is always a high price to pay for things of eternal significance. I think that deep down inside, we who are believers understand this intersection of our humanity and spirituality, but it does not always comfort us in the middle of our seasons of affliction. Take a full look at any great man, or woman of God in the Scriptures, and you will notice that before the joy and the triumph, there was also a time of great trial, and long periods of waiting in obscurity.

We live in an age where everything imaginable clamors for our attention. At times, even good things can keep us so distracted that we often miss the better things. Unless we take time to come away from all the "noise" and "distractions", we will never hear the still small voice of God whispering, "This is the way, walk ye in it." The human heart is rebellious and easily deceived. Given the freedom to move at will without constraint, our heart will always lead us in ways that are contrary to the desires of God. We must "put the brakes on" at times and separate ourselves from the natural pull of the world long enough to ensure that we are still in range to hear the sound of His voice. For this reason, we need time in solitude to establish a reference point in our lives. We need to make sure that the signs we are following are really leading us to the desired destination. God has an agenda that He wants to accomplish through our lives, but the Evil One, and even our own heart, is always offering counterfeit substitutions that can lead us off the intended path. I found myself on one of those counterfeit paths last year. I was almost certain that my greatest contribution to a fallen world would take place behind an educator's desk. I love people, and I love to teach. I figured the path I was on made perfectly good sense until my wife and I entered a season of intense financial and emotional strain. We had loved visiting the Duluth, Minnesota area and we felt that the town seemed like the most logical place to move after our son graduated from high school, but somehow I began to feel a check in my spirit that would not let me feel at peace with the move. We had prayed about it, and God had not given us a green light, but He also had not thrown any obvious roadblocks in our path. So, we took it as a "yes", and did not stop to consider whether it may have been a "no" or a "wait." We had been restless; anticipating a change of scenery without realizing the grass was pretty green from the side of the fence we were straining our necks over.

I will not bore you with all the details of our year and a half in the crucible, but it is sufficient to say that we learned a big lesson about waiting for God's clear direction, and perfect timing. By the end of the first year in Duluth we were nearly crushed, financially and emotionally. We were stuck in a corner because of an odd lease agreement, and the stress was compounded by a financial drought. Most of the college students vacated town during the summer, taking what little was left of an already struggling economy. We were in trouble, and we knew only one thing we could do about our situation. We went to our knees and begged for guidance and provision. We knew that the same God, who had brought us through such a trying year, would also make a way for our future. It seemed like the prayers were still leaving our mouths when the phone rang. I was surprised when I answered the call and heard my brother's voice on the other end of the phone line. He was curious to see if I had made any plans for the summer, and wondered if I would want to join him on a renovation job that he had named, "The North Shore Project." My wife and I were elated to receive his timely call, and we thanked God for His amazing timing. I had no idea at the time how far reaching; "The North Shore Project" would prove to be. We continued to praise God for His intervention in our hopeless situation, and prayerfully began planning for this change we would experience in our lives.

The following Monday, my wife and I shared an emotional time of saying, "good bye." We were not only sad, but also anxious about being apart. The trials of the previous year had welded us together, and we were not separating very easily. I would be working away from home on the project for up to a week and a half at a time. My wife would be spending much of that time alone during the evenings, since we had no family, or close friends living in the area that she felt comfortable being alone with. I struggled with the mixed feelings. On one hand I was grateful for the opportunity, but on the other hand I could not understand why it seemed like God's path for us at the time appeared to lead in two different directions. I was very concerned for my wife's emotional welfare, since we had been under such incredible stress over the past year. Nevertheless, the leading was unmistakable, and I was sure that God had a perfect reason for every decision He was making for our lives. The questions kept circling in my mind as I drove north on Scenic Highway 61. The only way I can describe my feelings that day is that I felt a little lonely, but comfortably at peace with the whole situation.

It was calming to drive away from the town that had been the source of perpetual turmoil for over a year. The forest, the flowers, and the occasional windows of lake view that opened between the trees, quieted my mind and flooded my weary soul with a gentle assurance. I found myself praying, and thanking God for the new adventure He had set before me. I prayed for the needs of my wife that she would be comforted by His Spirit and drawn into a deeper relationship with Him during our absence from each other. I prayed that God would somehow meet me in tangible ways during this season of seclusion, and reveal Himself to me in ways I had never recognized Him before.

The weeks and months to follow would be a series of fresh encounters that would become the foundations for this book; if not an entirely new creative mindset for everything I intend to write in the future. I have found that God still speaks with a "still, small voice," but sometimes He has to separate us from all of the "noise" in our lives that hinders us from hearing. I had always thought that in order for God to do a deep work in our hearts we had to be put on our backs with some sort of illness. Now, I am finding that God is never bound to the same method when He works in the lives of individual believers. He knows what it takes to get our attention, and this does not always have to be a negative thing that crushes us physically to make the desired impact.

As I have mentioned, my door of discovery has been solitude. It has been the slower pace that has allowed me to remember the "former things." He has shown me where His hand was leading in the past, where his feet were walking close to mine during the times when I assumed that he was a million miles away. He has shown me that every prayer was heard, every tear was bottled, and my groans were only extensions of His own. He has shown me that the stillness of solitude, the thing I have avoided most, would be the very thing that would transform my weary heart, for it is in the stillness that we can meet with our Lord and experience undisturbed fellowship, alone. It is during the times of stillness that the distractions of life, like a veil, are lifted away and His face becomes clearly visible.

The trials of life can sometimes distort our view, as we perceive Him solely through our circumstances. However, the security and stillness of solitude enables us to view our troubles through His eyes, and not just our own. Once we are safely hidden in the cleft of his hand, the fog lifts and we are able to see a different view of His face. His eyes become those of a lover, and His heart whispers, "Rise up my love, my fair one and come away" (Song of Solomon 2:10).

Once again, the Lord is courting and wooing as the Lover, healing and comforting as the Great Physician, and always leading as a Gentle Shepherd. I am finding that circumstances, like working on the "North Shore Project," are not always just about the work of our hands. Each project or circumstance the Lord guides us into is only a small segment of an even greater work He is doing in the hearts of everyone in the circumstance that is involved, not just one individual. My ears are beginning to hear, and my eyes are beginning to see a magnificent project that has only been set in motion this side of eternity. I am thankful for the renewal that took place in my heart, and the hearts of others who were working on the remodeling project. I am thankful that the experience opened a new door for my writing ventures, but even as great as these blessings are, I have not even approached the fringe of what God is up to in the bigger scheme of things. In reality, we are all His projects and the story He is writing will take our breath away. Some future day we will discover our lives written on the lines and pages of His book, and the stories may not seem to make sense individually, however, when joined collectively, they will be an eternal masterpiece we will never tire of reading.

Chapter Two

~Challenges~

*"It is God who arms me with strength and keeps my way secure.
He makes my feet like the feet of a deer; he causes me to stand
on the heights."*
~ Psalm 18:32,33

Some see mountains as opportunities; others see them as merely obstacles. As you read through the Scriptures you will notice that some of the greatest accounts recorded, took place upon mountains. Not everyone was allowed to ascend the mountains and take part in what was happening. Only those who had already drawn near to God in the valleys were ready to meet with Him on the peaks. Yes, the mountains with their breathtaking views and majestic peaks have always been symbolic of reaching up to God. We relish the stories that focus on the glory encountered in high places, but we sometimes overlook the sacrifice required in getting there. For a lot of folks, the mountain is nothing more than an impasse standing between where they are, and where they wish they could go. The climb appears to be too steep, so they make a detour from the path and head for smaller hills. They do not realize that the reward they forfeited would have been greater than the sacrifice, had they not turned away. For every one of the treasure-laden summits that present a challenge, there also comes a crisis of faith. This is a time of counting the costs– is it worth the risks and the suffering to lay hold of the treasure at the top? Sometimes, the very obstacles that we transcend in the present, equip us for even greater challenges and greater rewards in the future.

My brother has always loved a challenge, "The greater the challenge, the greater the payoff," he would say with a grin. He models the old saying," It's not the size of the dog in the fight; it's the size of the fight in the dog." He may look like the average dog, but inside his chest beats the heart of a grizzly bear. His heart has been enlarged by the many peaks and valleys he has traversed. On my good days, since I am likening our courageous virtues to those of bears and dogs, I'm a yellow lab-collie mix; on my bad days a poodle-terrier. I am hoping that by the time this project comes to an end some of my brother's "grizzly-ness" will rub off on me. The day I arrived was not one of those days when a deep, guttural growl would rumble from my snarled lips. The poodle emerged as I stood there staring at the lodge, realizing the enormity of our task. All of my sugary prose about mother's cinnamon rolls and sun-baked pine needles, fancifully imagined on the access road, somehow melted in my mind and oozed into the nearby lake. This was not my idea of, "doing a little shingling," as my brother had so casually mentioned on the phone. This qualified as a mountain and every square inch of its peaks had to be covered with shingles.

We discussed some of the particulars over lunch until we heard the sound of a big boom truck jarring through potholes on the access road. The truck driver jumped out and flashed a quick smile that disappeared just as quickly when he had a chance to survey the surroundings.

"Something wrong," we asked?

"Well, I got kind of side-tracked looking at the scenery coming down that hill.

It was sure easy getting into this place, but now that I'm in, I'm not sure if I'll be able to get out," he said with a frown of apprehension.

I assured him that I knew exactly how he felt. My brother smiled a knowing grin to let me know that he had felt my jab, and then put his gloves on. We climbed the ladder and took our places on the roof. The driver maneuvered the truck as close as he could without tipping over the hill on the west side of the lodge. He hopped out of the cab and stationed himself between the truck and the lodge. Then, he started playing with the remote controls to plant the outriggers, which he hoped would balance the load properly. The lodge has a small suspension bridge in front of it, and the pallets of shingles would need to be lifted over it at a great distance from the center of gravity on the truck. Fortunately for us, the remote controller had a manual override switch for the computer, and the operator was just crazy enough to experiment with it. The boom would only go out so far, and then the buzzer would go off, warning that an unsafe extension distance, given the weight of the pallets, had been reached. The pallets bobbed up and down over the ravine and the driver's stomach seemed to follow suit at times. We had our own hazards to contend with since the roof was not finished yet. One idle step carrying the shingle packs, and a guy could easily trip. Once you start falling on a roof like the one that is on the lodge, there is not much you can do, but start praying on your way down. Two hours later, the last pack of shingles was slammed down on the roof and it was time to take a well-earned break.

The sun was setting on the lake's endless skyline. An eerie thing happens on Lake Superior during this time of day during the summer months. As the air begins to cool, water vapors coalesce above the surface of the lake and they rise up in columns, like phantoms taking a late afternoon stroll. The experience is quite exhilarating after you have been working in the heat for several hours and then, one of those cold, ghostly plumes glides over your sun burned skin. We sat on the stacks of shingles and soaked in the incredible views. It was a chance to revel in the early rewards for undertaking such a monumental task. A thought crossed my mind– while you are down on the ground, all you can see is the size of the obstacle looming over you, but once you commit to the challenge, engaging in the first struggle, then your view about everything changes as your heart gets in sync with the grand scheme of things. It is sort of like pre-game jitters. Before the first whistle, all you can focus on is your nerves. You feel cold and clammy, and your heart pounds in your chest. Then, you make your first basket, or smack helmets with a player from the opposing side, and all the anxiety and adrenaline disappears when you realize that you are in the game.

As I looked around from the rooftop of the lodge and saw the incredible beauty of the rocky shoreline that extended far into Canada, I realized that, "I was in the game," and suddenly, my view of the work had changed. I could not believe I was being compensated to work in such a place. It sort of seemed like being commissioned to retile the stairway to heaven –the farther you get along in your work, the better the surroundings become. My brother had been telling me about a place that allows you to come and work for a small additional fee instead of paying the full price to stay at their resort. The audacity struck me offensively at first, but as I considered my own change of attitude, I realized that those resort owners were not too outlandish to charge for such an opportunity. As I realized my good fortune, a sacred hush fell over me, and a heart full of weary apprehension was replaced by one of anticipation and gratitude.

Most contractors would die for an opportunity to work at such a picturesque job site on the North Shore. Most of the time they are grinding it out at the same cookie-cutter housing developments and the scenery never changes from week to week. Here we were, working in a place that did not look like it had changed much since God designed it millennia's ago. The wildness of it all was making me feel more like a prowling grizzly than a whiny poodle (no offense intended to you poodle lovers). I started to catch a vision of how grand the lodge would look with the new roof over it. I could see all the happy guests that would come and share the awe that I had felt as I stared out across the miles of natural splendor. My sacrifice of sweat would provide a protective covering for folks that would come, hoping to find time alone with God.

I thought of Jesus, who faced a struggle with such magnitude none of us can ever possibly comprehend, or come close to experiencing. His eyes were not on the sacrifice He would make on Calvary, but on the joy that would follow. What was the basis of His joy? His joy came from knowing that His painful death, and the grave that would follow, was not the end of the story. He would ascend the heights and take His lofty throne after He had provided a covering for us so that we could come and share in His inheritance. He took our pain and punishment, because we never could have finished the job even if we were qualified to undertake it in the first place.

Why does it seem like there is always an obstacle to overcome in life before you can get to the good stuff? I think the obstacles are placed there to screen out the half-hearted who do not truly value the treasure that is being offered to them. It is all part of a delayed gratification thing. If the reward comes first, then the "carrot" becomes obsolete, and without the "carrot" there is no motivation to endure. There are many things in life that require endurance; in fact our survival often depends on it. And so, the reward only goes to those who endure, because only those who endure have proven their faith.

I am beginning to understand the relationship of reward and struggle a little better. It must be the clean air fueling my critical thinking faculties. I have a feeling the Lord wants me to spend a little time here. That conclusion is one that did not require much deliberation. There will be rewards, but I am sure they will not come easily. Nevertheless, I have to keep in mind that not all rewards come in the shapes that we expect them to. Part of the thrill is letting God select our rewards, and the appropriate time for us to receive them. If we knew everything ahead of time, we might be tempted to minimize the value of the reward, or we might miss something God desires to build into our character. What God chooses for us may not seem appealing at the present, but it will prepare us for the future, where greater challenges and still greater rewards are to be had. We have to trust His timing and goodness, knowing we will be the better for it. The Scriptures say that every good and perfect gift comes down from our Father in Heaven, no snakes or scorpions, but bread–the substance of life. I am hungry for more of that bread, that hunger is what drew me here in the first place. That hunger for more of His "bread" is the impetus behind almost everything I do. He gives me the hunger in my heart, and then I start sniffing my way towards the aroma, my "carrot," if you will.

The roof was a monstrous task, and I cannot say I was sorry when the last shingle went into place. My son had come to help with the shingling, and that was a blessing in its own right. It was quite the experience, my brother, and my son, the three of us grunting and sweating, struggling to finish the job. There were squashed fingers, peeled skin, blistered feet, and a few close calls, but there was also joyous laughter, lessons learned, sound sleep, peaceful rooftop sunsets, and plenty of "bread" to go around. We walked away from the roofing job a little lighter, if not around our waists, certainly in our step.

When you finish a huge task like shingling a lodge roof, the growl in your stomach comes back. To your delight, you soon find that even the most strenuous, tedious tasks are nothing to be feared, but actually challenges that affirm who you are as a man. A man with bad blisters, leg cramps, and pulverized thumbs, but a man nonetheless. With our mountain shingled, and put behind us, we were ready to move on to more pleasurable tasks. The days that lay ahead of us would be like walking down the backside of a mountain into the valley below, but there are also many troubles in the valley. There are pits strewn along the way; deep, dark, pits that a person cannot climb out of alone, and represent just as much of an obstacle as a mountain. The difference between the two obstacles is that a mountain's enormity compels a person upward; a pit on the other hand, operates exactly the opposite as the victim is drawn down and inward. When you are held captive in a pit, your vision is drastically limited and your dilemma is all that you can see. Nevertheless, that issue is reserved for another chapter and we will take that up, then.

Chapter Three

~Squirrelly Notions about Faith~

"If that is how God clothes the grass of the field, which is here today and tomorrow is thrown into the fire, will he not much more clothe you—you of little faith?"
~ Matthew 6:30

*M*y feet are warming next to the woodstove, which is crackling with burning boughs of cedar and birch. White caps are dashing against the rocks outside my window and I suddenly become aware of just how peaceful it is in this little cabin. The good doctor that owns this secluded resort has affectionately and adventurously named the little cabin I am staying in, the "Shackleton" after one of history's greatest explorers.

The "Shackleton," that is an interesting and thoughtful name for a cabin that stands against punishing gales, driving snow, and the sub-zero temperatures of Lake Superior winters. The cabin is nestled among Norway Pines, and hedged protectively by Aromatic Cedars, making it seem not so alone in the cold, misty seclusion. The weather is so fickle here in the North Land. Yesterday, I was comfortable working in short sleeves; tonight I hear icy snow racing across the brittle shingles above my head. The biting elements this night make me grateful to be inside of this warm little cabin where I am safe from the snow, the tethers of civilization, and the frosty waves that pound behind my head... at least for now.

You have to be a strange breed of person to enjoy such simple solitude as this. I am beyond the service of my cell phone. The one television on the property barely picks up a single channel, and that is only during favorable conditions. I have no computer with me to distract my attention, nor do I hear any voices projecting through the walls from any neighbors. There are no car horns, or blasting stereos.

I feel melancholy suddenly, not because of the silence and solitude, but because something of great value has been lost... this used to be the way of life for most people. That is until greed, and the seduction of mechanized industry called them out of the woods and rolling fields. Now we, not the work animals, are the beasts tethered by a leash. We can never wander too far from the feeding trough of civilization. Our bills and our bank accounts are like the invisible umbilical chords of a possessive mother who refuses to let us venture beyond the back yard. We left the forest and countryside with dreams of a better life, and now we have garnered for ourselves everything we could possibly want in our concrete cages–except our freedom.

So, how does one go about severing those umbilical chords? Well, that thought has been crossing my mind a lot lately. It is not that I dislike people, I love them, but I hate what happens when too many people are pressed into too small an area without sufficient resources. No, I love people, but I just need some space, space to call my own, a space to step off when I feel like I am going to be slung out of the centrifuge of society. We all need space to live, space to rest, a wide-open space with room to maneuver and meet with God.

I was somewhat distracted from my work today thinking about such wide-open spaces, so I surmised that another distraction would not really lessen my productivity. A movement had caught my eye. A little pine squirrel was quickly sorting his stores atop a fallen log. He seemed to be taking inventory and checking the quality of his winter fare. Every once in a while he would pull a cone from the pile and try a little bite. It is quite a sight to watch these little fellows feeding on pinecones that are almost as big as their body. They seem almost human as they hoist a pinecone to their mouths in much the same way that a human savors an ear of sweet corn. Their powerful little jaws work the cone, biting through the tough outer layer to uncover the treasure within. Once they extract the edible seed they spew out the chaff like a baseball player spitting the spent casings of sunflower seeds.

I envy my little friend's freedom. He is not trapped by the demands of any society, nor is he dependent on other creatures for his survival. God opens His generous hands and little creatures everywhere, like the squirrel, take just what they need. It is not a handout or laziness, because the little squirrel still has some work to do before he can fill his belly. It is more like opportunity. The squirrel has a need; God is quite aware of the need and makes provision. Nature works the way it is supposed to, and both the squirrel and God are pleased with the outcome. Squirrels are not concerned about unemployment rates, housing market crashes, recession, or food shortages.

I could not find many negative aspects about the lifestyle of my furry little friend other than he did seem to be a little greedy, hoarding all of his pinecones into mounds around the clearing. But, then I reconsidered as I remembered that very soon the harvest would come to an end when all the remaining pinecones would be frozen solid beneath the ice and snow, which is another principle I see – when God gives us opportunities we should take them while the window is open, for ***today's*** provision is not tomorrow's. Jesus taught us to pray, "Give us this day, our daily bread." When we get our bread for each day, and not for the whole week, it teaches us to stay dependent on God for our provision. His provision is a gift, not an entitlement. It is a stewardship principle; nature illustrates this principle most efficiently as the creatures are driven by survival, and not greed.

I admire the squirrel's ambition; he is a fascinating creature to watch. He uses his cheeks like saddlebags to transport his stores. Back and forth he scurries all day long, as the piles get smaller, and smaller. He seems to be taking his winter fare beneath the large deck of the main cabin. He is quite the thrifty character; making use of ready-made shelter. Earlier this week, we spotted him wadding long strands of pink insulation into his puffed cheeks. He would stuff his mouth full, and then disappear beneath the deck surface. We assumed that he must

have been using the insulation to chink the walls of his nest. It
was really comical to watch him running across the ledge with
long strands of pink insulation trailing both sides of his head
like a pink, cotton candy beard.

I wonder if animals can tell time. Right about the time
I would take a coffee break and hang up my tool pouch, it
seemed like the squirrel had similar ideas. I leaned back
against the wall and watched him climb up the big spruce
tree in front of the cabin. He perched himself on a limb about
twenty feet off the ground and went to work on a couple
of pinecones. Occasionally, he would bark challenges into
the frosty morning air, but no one seemed to notice besides
me. Earlier I had seen a pair of eagles flying low over the
treetops in the direction of the Canadian border. I assume
that they would prey on squirrels if given an opportunity, but
they were probably just scouting for fish, or waterfowl in the
cove around the bend. Maybe the dark shadows of the eagles
soaring overhead had provoked the little squirrel's attitude.
He seemed to be a little skittish every since they passed by.

I am not sure how much time I spent watching my little
friend, but I assure you the time was not wasted, because I
have learned some profitable lessons. The eagles have returned
and are roosting on their platform atop the highest spruce
tree on the ridge. I sure wish I could get a picture of them
landing. Stillness is now looming over the darkening forest. I
breathe deeply the crisp winter air; pure and invigorating like
the dark blue sky and bright stars appearing overhead.

Once again, I find myself pondering the squirrel. He has
taken shelter for the evening. He has the common sense
to know when he has accomplished enough for one day.
Is it a fear of the approaching darkness, or has he heeded

the warnings of the great horned owl? Does he secure the entrance of his nest, tidy the insulated walls, and then begin to worry if he has left anything undone, or fret about any miscalculations he might have made concerning his monthly rations? I doubt it. I picture him yawning and stretching his tired, little legs. One yawn, maybe two at the most, and he is fast asleep dreaming about the bounty of pinecones that he will discover tomorrow. I cannot help but wonder if our Heavenly Father is watching that little squirrel as he sleeps peacefully, and maybe wishing that the rest of His creation could learn to relax the same way.

The next time you get a chance, watch a squirrel's activity for a while. You might learn a few things about living a life of productivity while remaining at rest. No one knows exactly what tomorrow will bring, and there is really nothing we could do about it if we did. We were all meant to live one day at a time, not failing to plan for the future, but not borrowing any trouble from it, either. One of the most basic things we must learn to do is trust our good and gracious God, whose eye is on the sparrow, the little squirrels, and the rest of creation, which includes you and me. We can trust His care and provision. We can learn to rest and focus on the beauty and blessings of each new day, rather than letting worry steal our joy. Jesus told us to consider the lilies, which are clothed with more splendor than King Solomon was in all his glory. He also told us to consider the sparrows, which neither toil nor sow, but are fed by the Father. I have watched the sparrows and I have considered the lilies, but now I have learned some things from squirrels, and they are not as squirrely as I had once thought them to be.

Chapter Four

~Fear Not~

"Peace I leave with you; my peace I give you. I do not give to you as the world gives. Do not let your hearts be troubled and do not be afraid."
~ John 14:27

Fear not! Jesus used those two words so many times throughout the Gospels that we should have no doubt how He felt about the issue. Is it really true though, that we should never fear? Never fear, anything? Just try that for one day and see how you do. I'm thinking back over my day, and I am really surprised at how many times I've been confronted by fears.

The phone rang early this morning and I thought about a source of tension that has been hounding my wife and me for the past couple of months. When I finished my course work I quickly turned off the computer so that I could finish packing for the trip back to the North Shore. I needed to leave quickly, or I would be stuck in the afternoon traffic. As I walked to the car I had to stop and think for a second about my course work. Had I finished everything? I was certain that there was something that I was forgetting. I put the last of the luggage in the trunk and closed the lid. Again, I went through a mental checklist. I was not sure, but I could not help but feel like I had forgotten something that I would really need for the coming week up at the cabin. I pushed the thoughts out of my mind and drove as quickly as I could to get out of town.

Once I was on the road, I looked for a sermon I had downloaded, settled in for the long haul, and tried to concentrate on the message I was listening to. The sun was setting and it was a beautiful evening, clear and cool. I only had about fifty miles left to drive when I rounded a curb at a fairly high speed. The flash of a deer's eyes illuminated in my headlights, and you just never know what the deer are thinking right at a moment like this. They tend to go with the last thought that was on their mind before they were startled. I focused all my attention on the deer standing in the left side ditch, anticipating that any second she could lunge in an attempt to make it across the road. I had failed to notice the deer that were crossing from the right side. Out of the corner of my right eye I saw a flash of white as my high beams locked on the ghostly figure of a doe that was bounding toward the passenger side of my car. I swerved left to miss the doe on the right side, and to my horror, the doe on the left side shot forward. I slammed on the brakes and cranked the steering wheel to the right to avoid the first deer. The second one sprung over the hood of my car, narrowly avoiding a terrible collision. I have seen what is left of the deer and the driver when a deer goes through a car's windshield. Let me give you a hint as to what happens– a seat belt does absolutely no good, aside from holding your headless body upright in the seat. Thankfully, I did not lose my head in the situation, and neither did either of the deer. It was a clutch play by my guardian angels; an absolute miracle that I did not hit at least one of the deer. The whole incident lasted for about a second, but my hands were shaking and my heart was pounding for the remaining hour that I drove down the dark, secluded highway. My eyes were glued to the tree line, watching for any other deer that might try to cross the road.

It is strange how a close call like that can breed more fears as the day progresses. Maybe, it is an after effect of having a major adrenaline rush. Back in the woods where I have been working, it is almost pitch black at night unless the moon is overhead. One bad thing about arriving after dark is that there are several things that must be done before turning in for the night. The first thing is to restock the woodbin so you can build a fire in the stove. In my haste I had left the flash light on the dresser, and now I would have to carry the firewood down a very dark trail to my cabin. If it were the middle of January this would not really bother me, most of the bears are tucked in, and hibernating for the winter. Nevertheless, because we live in Minnesota, during this time of year the bears get confused when the temperatures fluctuate and there are good things still left around in the woods to eat. I know you are thinking about berries, and apples, but I was talking about guys that venture out to get firewood in the middle of the night without flashlights. These revelations never come to me while I am twenty feet from the cabin door. They normally come to me when my hands are full of wood on the return trip, and a twig snaps in the dark about twenty yards away.

Last spring we had an old bear that liked to tip over our dumpster every night to see if we had left him any treats during the day. It seems that he was always disgruntled that he had not found anything appealing at the top. Evidently, he was either too short to climb into the dumpster, or so large that turning it completely over and shaking all of its contents out seemed like an easier option. I found a large specimen of his excrement just recently on the hillside, so I was sure he hadn't forgotten his snack time routine. The unnerving thing was that I would have to carry my firewood right through the area where he likes to stroll around at night. These are the kind of thoughts you have when fear has been sticking close to your heels all day.

Some of the fears that I have been writing about may seem out of the ordinary for most folks. I must admit that I had more than my normal share today, but there is another type of fear that can creep in that can be a lot more troublesome. Sometimes, this fear does not go away. I am talking about the kind of fear that leads to depression, anxiety disorders, and despair. This is the kind of fear that the Evil One brings our way, and causes us to doubt. Doubt our salvation. Doubt the Lord's goodness. Doubt that our circumstances, or we, will ever change. Doubt that God can perform a miracle in our lives, or that we even deserve one.

We can become so conditioned by our fears and doubts that it leaves us frozen in our tracks, wondering if God has forgotten us, or even worse, if He has given up on us entirely. Maybe there is some besetting sin in our lives, and we cry out to the Lord for deliverance, but time and again we find ourselves falling to the same temptations. This can go on for so long that we almost give up hope that we will ever be free, and now we feel that God has finally rejected us. Of course, the devil likes to remind us of how far we fall short. He has a devious way of baiting the traps we fall into, making them seem so appealing, but after we take the bait he quickly changes hats and becomes a ruthless prosecutor. He hangs over us like a dark cloud, enveloping us with shame and heaviness. A person grows weary as the cycle keeps repeating, and he wonders in his heart, "Where is God? When will He rescue me from my adversary? When will the battle ever end? When will I finally be free from this daily turmoil and agony of soul?" This, is where Jesus steps in and says, "Fear not." Do you know why He rebukes this kind of fear? He hates this kind of fear because it originates with one of Satan's lies. There is no reason to fear these lies. Jesus is a righteous judge, and He does not wink at sin, but He is also our advocate. He is the Supreme Court with no higher appeals for the prosecuting bench. No, He has the final say when it comes to justice and mercy, forgiveness and grace. He paid the price to own that privilege and He hates it when the devil deceives us into thinking that we have no hope of mercy, forgiveness, and transformation.

The fires of oppression can shape us, but they cannot destroy us. There is an intended result when we battle with certain oppressive fears. They are meant to drive us to the only One who can calm them. They are meant to strengthen our faith so that we will stand on God's promises and not by our feelings, especially those feelings that oppose the promises that God has made to us in His Word.

I heard a great story on the way up to the resort that deals with these types of self-doubts and fears from a woman speaking in one of my CD sermons. I think it was before my deer escapade, because I remember her story almost word for word. She happened to be talking about this very same mysterious struggle that so many of us have experienced in our walk with God. She told the listeners that her husband had found a house to buy. He had envisioned what a charming home it could be for their family after a few renovations. He seemed to be able to see exactly how the house would someday look as he relayed to her the vision he had for the place. She became excited as she listened to his description, and they went to the house so she could have a look around. When they arrived at the house she saw the same beauty and charm on the outside that he had spoken of, but her heart sank when she walked inside. She gulped as she looked about the house. Wallpaper was hanging in strips on the wall. Plaster was dangling from the ceiling. Some of the windows were cracked, or painted shut. The place was in shambles and the idea of trying to restore the old house seemed like too big a task to undertake. Her hopes had been dashed. Meanwhile, her husband was dragging her from room to room, telling her about everything he envisioned for the place. He would knock out a wall here, put some more windows in the living room and the upstairs, and build a breakfast nook off the kitchen. She could not get beyond the horrible condition the house was in and tried to talk him out of buying it. He could not be persuaded. He bought the house for a pittance and promptly went to work. He finished the rooms that she had wanted finished first so that she might be enticed to get behind the endeavor. Eventually, she caught the vision, and she was amazed at how the home had evolved into the exact image that her husband had described. He was not blind to the condition the house was originally in. He knew what a mess it was, but that was not what he focused on. He focused on what the house would some day become for the family, and that vision carried him through all the hard, sweaty work.

In God's eyes, that house represents our broken lives. He sees the inside of us, and yes, it is a mess, but someday it will not be when He is finished with our remodeling. We see our condition and we think, "We will never change enough to satisfy God's standards." We sink into despair believing that God would never want to tackle a project as difficult as we present. But He does, because someday you will look like His Son when His work in our lives is complete. The miracle is that you will hardly notice the changes that take place over time. That is, until one awesome day when we will all take a look back and see what God was up to when we did not think anything was even happening, or even possible.

Noline Rhodes of Time Square Church in New York City was the speaker's name, and I will give her credit for such a comforting analogy. I find the analogy so comforting, because it sure seems like the Lord has been working on my house for a long time. Nevertheless, that is why we sometimes become discouraged. We look at other people's internal remodeling project and wonder how theirs was finished so quickly. You never know, maybe they will be used for storage, but you and I will be a place the Lord likes to come and kick back because He spent so much time with us during the renovation. Maybe

He's taking extra time on you and me so He can glory in where He brought us from, and the perfection He can see in the finished product. He makes all things beautiful in His time, even us "broken down shacks. "

Well, I did make it back to the cabin without running into the dumpster dumping bear. My feet sure feel good warming by the fire as I transfer my thoughts onto paper. The deer that I almost collided with are probably both reclining on some grassy hillside waiting for the moon to rise so they can go forage for something to eat. They are probably undisturbed by the fact that some guy, preoccupied with analogies between remodeling an old house and the inner workings of the Holy Spirit, almost turned them into hood ornaments. My wife checked my sent files and confirmed that I did indeed send all the required course work, where it is now resting in my professor's inbox, awaiting review. Bummer! I forgot my toothbrush. See, I knew there was good reason to fear something. Now I'm going to have to drive to town and buy one, or maybe not. There really is no one out here to offend with my morning breath anyway, and hey, I really have been enjoying the simpler, more rustic way of life.

It is pretty warm in my cabin now, and hopefully it has thawed my bed out enough to sleep in it. I am looking forward to the remodeling I will be doing on the main cabin tomorrow. As I turn in for the night, I am thinking about Jesus' command, "Fear Not." That is good advice, you know! It is coming from some One who has been down the road you are traveling, and He knows where all the hidden dangers are around the bend. And what is more, He knows how to get you where you are supposed to go. He knows what renovations He wants to do in your heart, and what you will look like when His work is finished. He is down at the end of the road waiting for me, and He is waiting for you. He never takes His eye off us, even in the dark where grouchy old bears might be waiting, whether in reality or only in children's imaginations. Since we can never escape His thoughts or His watchful eye, then what do we have to fear?

Relax and, "Fear not."

Chapter Five

~Blessings-Count Them~

"Who, then, are those who fear the LORD? He will instruct them in the ways they should choose. They will spend their days in prosperity, and their descendants will inherit the land."
~ Psalm 25: 12,13

*M*y brother and niece just arrived. As much as I love the solitude of this hidden retreat, I am also delighted to share the blessings with the people I love. The first night we are all back at the resort is a treat. It is normally too late in the day to start working, so we sit around the fire, eat popcorn, and share the latest family news. It is like getting into a time machine and coming out in another era, with no pressure from city traffic, pushy people, or work deadlines that cannot be met with some reasonable amount of effort. There is always another day for things that are not finished today. Out here the day's tasks are discussed over a cup of hot coffee, hash browns, fried eggs, sausage links, and a steaming stack of pancakes. I know you are thinking, "How do you get any work done after a breakfast like that?" Well, it does take a little determination, but we ease into things slowly, and eventually build up enough steam to make some progress.

We usually start the day with what we call a "warm-up." A warm-up is a task that is not directly related to making progress on the renovation work, but it is a task we enjoy and find necessary to the function of the place. A warm-up helps you get limbered up for the real work. My "warm up" for this morning was restocking the fire wood supply for the cabin we are working in. The cabin comes equipped with a beautiful, Ben Franklin wood stove that we are very fond of. In fact, so fond that we have been known to fire it up on warmer days, just to create a rustic aura. Those old stoves take awhile to heat up, but they also take awhile to cool down. Our dad says that when you have a blazing stove like the old Ben Franklin, you about have to use the front door as a thermostat. The other alternative is working in your boxer shorts, which looks pretty silly with a carpenter's belt and snow boots.

I used the resort's handy little pull cart to haul my wood from the pile. The firewood company delivered our wood on an old logging truck that has a "cherry picker" boom. It is amazing to watch those guys unload a year's supply of wood in about 20 minutes. Our order for this year was thirteen chords. The logs come in eight foot pieces, and then we pull them off the pile and on to the sawbuck for easy cutting. The stove holds twenty two-inch sticks of firewood, so I do have to cut and split quite a bit to keep our pile stocked. A friend of ours, and his father helped out a lot by bringing a hydraulic log splitter to give us a hand. The two of them split about seven chords in one day. A pile like that looks like it would last all winter, but when the temperatures sink to thirty below, old Ben can really eat up the wood in a hurry. It did not take long to finish my "warm up" today. I split and stacked a half chord of wood in front of the cabin. I love working with firewood, but now it is time to get going on the productive work.

Today, it feels pretty bitter with the misty wind coming off the lake, so I decided to do some prep work for a future day when the conditions are not so raw outside. We would need to cut strips of tarpaper to put on the roof additions once they are completed, so I figured that would keep me busy for a while. I stoked the stove and got it going really hot, and then spread the rolls of tarpaper out on the cabin floor where they could warm up, making them easier to handle and cut. It took a few hours to cut the strips, and by then I decided that I needed a break from the heat. Working in all that heat really works up an appetite. So, I took leave of my project and wandered down to the main lodge to make some lunch for the three of us. I wear a lot of different hats at this construction site, which is good, because more hats means more versatility. If there is a task that I am not found handy while wearing a carpenter's apron, I redeem myself wearing a cook's apron. Being versatile is a blessing, and that is another one, if you are counting them, too.

For lunch we are having a thick version of my sausage gumbo. I take a box of red beans and rice, a package of spicy, sizzle and serve savory sausage links, try saying that five times fast, a packet of onion soup mix, and a box of boil in the bag brown rice blend to stretch things out a little bit. Before long, the aroma of my spicy, Cajun creation was permeating every cranny of the lodge.

While the gumbo was gumbo-ing in the pot, I thought I would wash the breakfast dishes. Snow was beginning to fall on the hillside behind the lodge. Not the small variety of snow flakes, but the big feathery kind that seem to take their sweet time getting to the ground. I was tempted to gripe about the weather; because there were a few things I needed to do on the roof of the cabin. I had put the project off for lack of better reasons other than I thought we would have more good weather. It was only a couple of days ago that we were working in warm sunshine wearing short sleeves. A cold front had taken an unsuspected ninety-degree turn in its northerly path and decided to come south a few hundred miles to pay us a visit. Now, here we are checking the trunks of our cars to see if we remembered to thrown in the winter weather gear. Nevertheless, I will hold firm to my belief, as the Apostle Paul did, that all things do work together for good for those who love God and are called according to His purposes. We would be in sitting by the fire eating my "Cajun Creation Extraordinaire". So, for the present I had to believe that this really was for our good. Good food, good fellowship, and a good, warm fire. Hmm... that makes three more blessings, if you are counting.

My fellow renovators enjoyed the fiery dish; so much so that my brother has passed out, wrapped in the bearskin throw on the couch, he is fast asleep by the fire. My niece has gone back to her varnishing detail and now the lodge is quiet except for the occasional rumblings I hear coming from the bearskin on the couch. Maybe it is not a bearskin throw after all, judging from the sounds I hear. I am not sure if those are snores that I hear or something worse. It is hard to tell since I cannot make out which way the bear is facing.

While I was rinsing the pots, a movement on the hillside caught my attention. A yearling buck was grazing on what was left of the summer's raspberry bushes. He was so close that I felt like I could open the window and scratch behind his ears. I watched him grazing undisturbed and peaceful, at times raising his head for a quick glance to ensure that no danger was lurking close by. Winter here is really tough on the deer, especially the young, the sick, and the old. There are long stretches of sub-zero weather, heavy snowfalls, and limited food sources. Nevertheless, here was this porky little forager trying to pack on a few last minute pounds before facing the tougher months ahead. He eats contentedly with the mild snowfall circling about him.

It really is a miracle that the deer and other animals can survive here, facing such challenging conditions. Sometimes, we even take for granted God's provision for us. It is not that we are ungrateful, but it is so repetitive that we forget that each day's provision is a gift, and not something we are due. He really does care and provide for all of creation. Some would argue that this is not true. They believe that their paycheck puts the food in their belly, not God's kindness. However, I would argue that even a person's employment, and the store where he buys his food, is the providence of God, and something he should be thankful for. These are all blessings, though we do not often think of them as such. Are you still counting? Do you agree, or am I ahead of you in the day's tally?

Well, the little deer has moved on while I was counting my blessings. Yes, I will add him to the list too. God, that gumbo was good! I really mean that, "thank you God, the gumbo was really good. God you are so good! Thank you for the people in New Orleans that put together the spices. Thank you for the people who harvested the rice and beans. Thanks for the farmers who teamed up with the packing plant to make that great sausage. Thanks for a brother and niece who are better than best friends, keeping me company while I am away from my wife.

You see, when you spend all your days keeping an eye out for blessings you do not really notice too many negative things. If you expect good to come your way, more often than not, you will not be disappointed. It seems like an attitude of gratitude waters the seeds of fortuity that keep sprouting throughout the day. Call me superstitious and a bit optimistic if you will, but I believe God favors a grateful heart. There is great gain in having a contented heart. The Apostle Paul said that he had learned to be content in all situations whether he had much, or little. In fact, Paul wrote most of his epistles from a dingy prison cell. Even so, you can feel the enthusiasm in his writing. He was not worried so much about himself. He had faced so many hardships that he looked at every trial as a possibility to know the Lord better, and grow in character. Have you ever met anyone that rejoiced in his or her suffering? I think the only way you can rejoice in your suffering is if when you experience suffering you realize that it serves a positive purpose in the end. The only way to enjoy the good things of life is to also experience the bad, or how would you know what is good? Good would just be routine, and mundane. It is kind of like pudding after a plate full of broccoli. Sorry if you happen to be one of those weird people that just love broccoli. For you folks, I do not have a good analogy to use for a reference point. The key is to give thanks in all things, whether it is broccoli, **"hurray,"** or double chocolate, hot fudge pudding with a dollop of whip cream on top, "HURRAY!" Yes, it is okay to be more thankful for some things than others.

There are a few of us hearty type folks who enjoy living here in Minnesota year round. Very few, granted, but a few nonetheless. We do not necessarily relish four feet of snow in one night, forty below mornings, cars that will not start, fingers and toes that do not seem to function right until May, or February winds that leave your face feeling like it has been shredded by a cheese grater. No, we love being here, because we get to experience the full gamut of what the seasons have to offer. It is the contrast or disparity at different times of the year that enhance the quality and beauty of each season. When we grow weary of the grey skyline, and black, lifeless tree limbs, we know we can anticipate with great joy, the intensity of color and beauty that spring sends our way. It is in the spring that our dormant woodlands seem to explode with color and life. When it is so cold that breathing becomes difficult and you are chilled to the core, the experience of sipping a cup of hot chocolate by a warm fire moves into a whole new dimension of pleasure. Not so for the man or woman who endures nine months of ninety percent humidity and eighty-five degree average temperatures. When July temperatures sky rocket to near the century mark and it stays that way for two months, the first hint of fall, and the arrival of Jack Frost, makes even the grouchiest old codger as giddy as a schoolboy. The spring rains are cold and dreary, but then the summer lake breezes blow away the gray clouds and the water dances with sparkling sunlight. Just when the summer colors begin to fade, the flowers all droop, and the grasses wither and brown, the night chill paints the forest with spectacular arrays of orange, red, and yellow.

Nature is always in the process of change. Change is exciting. Change alleviates boredom and familiarity. Seasons of decline, give way to seasons of abundance. Seasons of cold, give way to seasons of warmth. Seasons of death, give way to a season of new life. Nothing really stays the same if you have a grateful heart; I know some post modernists say that there is never anything that is really new. I feel sorry for those folks; because they must not be seeing and experiencing the same things that we expectant, grateful people get to encounter afresh each day.

The very laws that we see at work in nature can be seen in our own lives, because they are established by the same Creator. We may experience a season where our creativity wanes and the once fertile fields of our productivity lay fallow. Not to worry, what has decayed will nourish what is to come. The chill we feel now will intensify the pleasure we feel when the first rays of sunshine greet us in our darkness. Are you counting your blessings, all of them, including both the pleasures and the problems? I could only find one negative thing about today, and that was the snow. Now I realize that I was wrong. I would have missed a great conversation with my brother. The gumbo would not have been nearly as comforting if it was as warm as it was yesterday. I may not have seen the little deer if he could have found a better place to graze than the hillside. And, now that the snow on my car has melted and slid off, I cannot believe how clean and shiny it is.

Tomorrow, try sowing some seeds of gratitude. Try to spot as many blessings as you can and I predict that you will have a hard time noticing as many negative things as usual. Or, better yet, maybe you will begin to see problems in a different light, and you will be able to double the number of blessings you can count. By the way, the next time the weather forecast is wrong and you get snow instead of sunshine, pick up a good box of spicy gumbo mix. It will keep you warm all day long, even if your attitude gets a little chilly at times. So, how many blessings did you notice in this chapter? Sorry, I lost count.

Chapter Six

~Down In the Hole~

"He lifted me out of the slimy pit, out of the mud and mire; he set my feet on a rock and gave me a firm place to stand."
~ Psalm 40:2

There are some things that simply must be done first in any remodeling project.

These are the tasks that you would rather put off until a more convenient time, but because the old must be stripped away before the new can be put in place, you have no choice but to grit your teeth and take care of first things first. I was not the first to go down in the hole, my brother was. I was in charge of demolition, so there were things that I needed to do first before we could start framing the new rooms and start restoring the outside of the cabin. My brother unfortunately had come to the point in his work where he could no longer avoid the inevitable. In order for the cabin to be functional during all four seasons, the plumbing and wiring would have to be replaced. Since there was no basement, and only a crawl space, we nicknamed it, "The Hole." Most of the plumbing and a good percentage of the wiring would have to be routed through that dreaded, dark pit. The "Hole" is a very dark, creepy, and dirty place. It is the kind of place that children, and now a couple of grown men, frequently have nightmares about. One simply cannot crawl through it without becoming tangled in decades of dusty spider webs. There are things in there that grow increasingly more evil the farther in you go. The air is foul, and not even a mask will completely protect you from the harmful particles and stray gases that seep up from the dank soil.

My brother is a hard worker, and he normally does not tire easily, but by the second week, I could tell something was taking a toll on him physically. Originally, what had been projected as taking only a few days at most was becoming one monster of a task due to the obstacles that he kept running into, and had to keep working around. The cabin was originally constructed in the 1930's. Not much attention had been given to clearing the ground in the crawl space. Originally, the cabin was built for summer use only. In the fall, the owners would blow out the water lines, and then lock it up for the winter. So, when they built the foundation they simply cut a track to pour the cement into, and they pushed the large boulders they found, and anything else that was in the track towards the center of the crawl space. When they framed the floor joists they tossed any left over wood scraps into the center, also. It was amazing what we found down in that dark hole. It would not have surprised me to find an old car, or possibly a tractor, or two. Navigating the maze of boulders and construction debris, while slithering on your back and stomach, is like trying to crawl out of a blast zone. With each movement, a thick cloud of red dust boils up, taking the breath right out of you. When the crawl space project stretched into the third week, I was wondering just how much more my brother could take. I tried to help him, but I did not fully understand the work that was being done, or where he was in the scheme of things. Most of the time when someone is in a situation like that, it is hard to help them; you just wind up getting in the way of what needs to be done. I had mixed feelings, I really felt bad for my brother, but I also must admit that secretly, I was relieved when he said that I did not need to go down there with him right at that time, it was "something that he had to do." So, I carried on with my work while he inched his way through the struggles he was facing down in the hole. Then, one day he was finished with his tour of duty in the dungeon and he emerged from the depths victorious. The old system was stripped away and the new was put in place. The cabin had a new heart and my brother's had been sorely tested. I remember the way he looked, as his face poked out from the access hole, not even the dirt, cobwebs, or grime could veil his radiant joy. He acted like a man who had been set free from a life sentence. He nearly skipped to the cabin door, urging me to quickly follow. He turned the yellow handle on the expansion tank, and then rushed to the kitchen sink. He proudly lifted the faucet handle and water gushed forth. We rejoiced with exceeding, great gladness. For three months we had been making the trip into town for potable water, and even the water used for cleaning had to be carried in five-gallon jugs from the well at the rear of the property. The old cabin had a heart transplant and a new lease on life.

I must admit that I enjoyed the adventure of living "pioneer style." My inventive side was put to the test on several occasions, but my most shining achievement was the shower system that I had constructed. The shower was of the gravity-feed type, my reservoir being a ten-gallon waste container that I had mounted on a crossbeam and then bolted to the side of the deck. I fabricated a shower stall using some old sheets from an extinct hotel. My water heater was a galvanized garbage can that tilted over a brick fire pit. I would heat the water to boil and then mix it half-and-half with cold water to get the right temperature. Then, the shower water was dumped into three, five-gallon buckets that I would then pour into my reservoir. The third bucket was a back up for a longer shower. The whole process took about an hour to complete each night, but it was well worth it. Nevertheless, like all improvisations, sooner or later, we humans take the path of least resistance, and I betrayed my pioneering heart by reverting to a shower of modern convenience, once it was available. The cabin was no longer just a shell of a building. It could now be inhabited because of the full accommodations. We had been roughing it for several months, so I figured that a few conveniences would be kind of nice for a change. Besides, I have to admit that the out door shower was getting a little too invigorating when the temperatures dropped below freezing at sunset.

With every victory comes a new challenge, and this marks the point where I would begin my season in "The

Hole." Running water is a blessed convenience, but the bad news is that water pipes in our neck of the woods have to be protected from the climate extremes. The nights were getting really cold and the foundation of the building was too drafty to hold any of the cabin's radiant heat. Now, I would get a chance to experience my brother's woes. I would find out what it is like to spend a lot of time down in the dark dungeon. My task would be to seal the foundation with foam board, and fill the floor joists with insulation. In addition to insulating the crawl space, an insulating cage would need to be built around the most sensitive areas where the small water lines and drains would run. After the cage was constructed, a small heat source would need to be installed that would heat just the cage, so as not to drive up the winter heating costs when no one was occupying the cabin.

To give you an idea of how cold it gets at the resort, it is only a short drive to the town of Embarrass, Minnesota which holds the record for lowest temperature in the lower forty-eight states, at nearly eighty below zero. Since the temperatures have dropped that low before, it is not out of the question that it could happen again. I would need to do a very thorough job of fabricating a solid barrier to the destructive temperatures the little cabin could possibly face. In fact, the work that was going on down in the hole was probably the most important work to be done on the entire cabin as it would be foundational to the possibility of offering year round lodging.

I began my work by crawling around the interior perimeter of the building, dislodging any large rocks and digging a track against the wall that the foam insulation panels could be wedged into. It is amazing how the years can solidify some of the rocks into place. After a while the soil dries out and acts almost like mortar. It would take me a great deal of time just to prepare the ground so that the real work could begin. After the track was completed, I cut twenty-eight inch square panels from the foam insulation board. They would be secured to the wall and mounted in the track.

I found that it was best to spend only two hours at any given time down in the crawl space, before crawling out to stretch and take in some clean air. The dark space in the hole can make you very claustrophobic, especially when some of the areas were pinched to less than eighteen inches of crawling space. After spending an hour sandwiched in impossible positions, you start thinking of worst case scenarios: *massive leg cramps, support footings that collapse because of decay and carpenter ant activity, a freak northern migration of poisonous snakes to this very location, wolverines, ancient burial grounds*, you know, some of the weird things that would probably never happen. A sudden sighting of a few small mice in such a confined space becomes as fearsome as running into a bear in your dark garage. Don't laugh; it happens all the time around here. Sooner or later, people learn to close their garage doors after dark and quit leaving apple pies to cool on the garage work bench. One silly lady opened the garage door and found a bear eating her pies that she had made for a church bake sale, and she decided to give it a sound thrashing with the first thing in reach? a sponge mop. The bear looked at her like,"You're kidding right?" Tossing the pies and the sponge mop aside, he decided her shoulder would be a better treat to sink his teeth into. She was able to successfully dislodge the bear by giving it a good poke in the eye. The news report did not elaborate as to whether the bear retaliated in like manner, maybe a head butt or something. Sorry, I lost focus for a minute.

By now you should fully understand why working in "The Hole" gave me the creeps. Insulating is not a very enjoyable task to start with, but in a crawl space it has to rate right up there with watching the recent state of the union address. All of the insulation bundles had to be crammed through the tiny access door, which was built for emaciated men that were just emerging from the Great Depression, not guys that start the morning with pancakes, sausages, hash browns, and eggs, it is small I am telling you, really small. Once I made it inside with the insulation, the individual pieces had to be pushed to the farthest corners of the crawl space using an eight-foot section of copper pipe. As you can imagine, the insulation fibers pick up everything from pine needles, cobwebs, fossilized mouse carcasses, all forms of decaying species of the microscopic animal kingdom, and yes, as much dirt as can possibly adhere to the insulation, until by some freak law of gravity, it is released when positioned directly over a human face. Once every bit of disgusting organic matter has fallen due to the strange law of gravity I discovered, then comes the added treat of glass fibers that magnetically attract to your eyes and the softest skin tissue of your neck. I found that I had discovered another hidden law of physics. I shall have to add these to the "Contractor's Bible of Strange Anomalies," an amendment to the popular book of, ""Murphy's Laws." I tried everything to make things more comfortable like goggles, long underwear, and stocking caps, but there was just no way of escaping the misery of working with insulation in such a case. I say all these things to make it clear to you, the reader, that you would be hard pressed to find a worse line of work than insulating a crawl space; shoveling pig manure, piece of cake; garbage collection, a walk in the park. Nevertheless, like the aforementioned, it is a job that must be done, no matter how trying it can be. You have been warned; so never quit your present line of work.

So, my brother developed pneumonia, and a host of other ills from his tour of duty in the insufferable crawl space. Even though I wore a ventilation mask, I went through a couple of days where I seriously thought I would be making a trip to the E.R. if I could have made it. The dust was bad enough, but we think the insulation was trapping some really foul gas fumes in the crawl space. It was indeed a glorious day for me when I finished the protective box for the plumbing, put in place the last piece of insulation, and crawled out of that "den of torture." Lying on your back for weeks in dark silence and tormenting conditions are fertile situations for deep thought. You really think about a lot of things. I know you are thinking, "How about a different job?" No, I finished that segment of reasoning the first day. I am talking about the days that followed. I believe that God has a purpose for everything we experience in life, and once again I find it amazing how certain circumstances can mirror what is going on down in our hearts. Trying circumstances allow us to see the work that is needed down in the dark, dirty recesses of our own hearts; down where nobody wants to go. It is much more pleasant to work on the exterior things, up where we can see the tangible work being done and can cover over the ugly, hidden things with superficial remedies. But superficial remedies just do not work, "down in the hole." A task left undone down there can be catastrophic when we are faced with the extremes that life sometimes blows our way. Sometimes, we have to go down into a dark pit so that we can help someone else, and share the same sufferings they experience. We might not have the really important work to do, the jobs that everyone can appreciate and deem necessary like replacing the plumbing or power supply. Perhaps, we will be required to continue someone else's work, or provide a protective barrier for someone's soul. Sometimes, the work can be miserable and thankless; we do not want to spend a day longer than absolutely necessary in that kind of darkness. However, the day finally comes when the work is finished at the core, at least until the project moves to another stage, and further work is needed down there.

It is quite a feeling to come through an ordeal like spending a long time in "The Hole," but you start to see the reasons in hindsight. You emerge from the dark pit a different person. The tasks that you had once thought of as boring and monotonous, like sweeping floors or washing dishes start to seem like a whole lot of fun. You develop a grateful heart for the little things, seeing any other kind of work as a gift, not drudgery. Do not get me wrong; I doubt that I will be searching the classified ads for crawl space insulator positions any time soon, but the struggle made me a better person, a better worker, and a more contented child of God.

Have you spent any time in a hole lately? It is dark in there, sort of scary, too isn't it? Maybe you have been down in that hole for a long time now. Are you flat on your back, wishing that you could find your way to the door where you entered your— time in "The Hole?" Keep this in mind— some of the most important work God may be doing might be taking place while you are in the darkest hole. Ask Him, "Why am

I down here? Please, show me what You want me to learn from this experience." Do not give up hope. Remember that in God's line of work, every thing has a season and purpose. He will not leave you down there indefinitely, or alone. "A friend is always loyal, and a brother is born to help in time of need" (Proverbs 17:17). I know it is dark, but you have to believe that He is at the heart of the project, equipping you to face any kind of weather, even eighty below zero.

There is just one more question that keeps surfacing in my mind— I wonder why they named the town, "Embarrass, Minnesota." All I can surmise is that maybe, all of the pipes broke, or the sewer pipes froze causing the toilets to back up, because nobody took the initiative to spend sufficient time down in the hole, that is just a guess. I will have to take a drive to that little town, and find a town historian that can answer that question for me.

Chapter Seven

~Deer Friends~

I will not fear though tens of thousands assail me on every side.
~ Psalm 3:6

knew that there were wolves inhabiting this region, but I did not realize just how close they ventured to the resort. I was driving to the nearest town for supplies today, and judging from the cars ahead, I figured that there must have been an accident of some sort. Some cars had pulled over on to the shoulder, and some were rolling along at barely a snail's pace with the hazard lights blinking to caution other motorists. I was not really sure what had happened since I could not see any banged-up cars in the ditch, or any rescue vehicles on the scene. One man was leaning across the hood of his car with his camera perched on a tripod taking pictures. What in the world was causing all the commotion? For a split second, two cars passed in the opposite lane from me, leaving about a twenty-yard window of view, and then I could see what had captured everyone's attention. A monstrous, silver, timber wolf was nonchalantly taking a morning jog through the ditch along the west side of the road. Every twenty feet, or so he would stop and look back at all of his adoring fans, and then jog on for a few more yards.

It was thrilling to see the old boy so close to a town. Perhaps, he was scouring the ditches looking for carrion. I wrote the incident off as a rare sighting, and carried on with my errands. When I arrived at the hardware store I found that the fame of the jogging wolf had traveled faster than I had. Someone was concerned that the wolf had been sighted so close to the school playgrounds. Others wondered if there would be more wolves venturing farther into town. I do not think that I have ever heard of wolves attacking small children on a playground, but I guess it could be a possibility.

It is this kind of incident that I find so comical about small towns— even the smallest incidents can make front-page headlines if enough people start talking about it, and they have the chance to embellish the details a little bit. By the time the news reaches the hundredth person, what initially was only a hungry timber wolf searching for road kill, can turn into a story of epic proportions. By the time the story reaches the local press, the story has been exaggerated to the point that the wolf has been on a killing spree devouring the second grade teacher, and at least half of her class before the National Guard was able to put down the horrific beast with a rocket propelled grenade. After the newspaper sells a record number of copies, a retraction is printed the following week explaining how the facts were stretched "somewhat".

As I waited in line to pay for my plumbing parts, I had to chuckle a few times as I listened to the newest eyewitness accounts that came from people who streamed into the hardware store thinking that they were the first on the scene with news of the wolf. Eventually, it was my turn to pay for my items, and the clerk and I exchanged knowing smirks. I bid her a good day, and waded through the throng of storytellers. The ruckus had slowed me down so much that I opted to finish a less time consuming project, attaching joist hangers that would support the floor underneath the front addition.

A few hours later, the sun began to set and the temperature was falling fast with it. I decided to call it a day and gather the night's firewood. In the distance, I could hear the sirens of an ambulance as it raced down the highway near the resort. The sirens seemed much louder than they probably were due to the deathly still, fall night. When the ambulance had passed and the sirens were almost beyond hearing distance, another high-pitched sound erupted in the darkness. Soon, there was a chorus of yelps and howling not more than three hundred yards from where I was standing in the woods. The hair on my neck stood up, because I knew it was not dogs or coyotes, it was the unmistakable, eerie howling of a wolf pack and there was no doubt in my mind that there were a lot of them. A cold chill swept over me as I grabbed the axe and took off running for the cabin and the illuminated clearing behind it. Suddenly, I was no longer mocking the concern of the local town's people about the wolf sighting. I heard a crashing, stomping sound at the top of the ridge. My heart pounded as I ran into the clearing and hurdled onto the patio deck with my eyes scanning the ridge to locate any movement. Then, I heard several snorts of white-tailed deer from different locations and it sounded like a stampede racing along the top of the hill. The peculiar thing is that they were not running from me, they were all running together to the east end of the ridge, tails like white flags bouncing in the shadows. There must have been fifteen to twenty deer, all bunched in a circle; stomping their feet and snorting in the direction from which I had heard the wolves howling. I had never seen so many of these local deer herded together at one time and my initial estimate of their numbers could have been way less. Where had they all come from? Had the wolves been trailing them to the bowl at the top of the ridge where they winter? I watched from the safety of the porch for quite some time as the deer paced at the top of the hill in circles, constantly stomping their hooves, sounding warnings, their necks stretched forward, ears attentive to any on-coming intruders. The smaller deer skittishly snuck to the rear of the herd and bunched together in small groups, heads bobbing alertly. Another round of yelps and howls erupted in the darkness, but this time the echoes came from farther away. Evidently, the wolves had ventured close enough to consider their odds against the herd, but found themselves out-numbered and moved on in hopes of finding a less challenging meal. One by one, the deer on the ridge dismissed themselves from the gathering and headed to the lakeshore for their evening drink. Content that the deer had disbanded and given the "all's clear," I resumed my activities gathering the firewood.

As I picked up the wood it gave me a chance to ponder what I had just witnessed. What could be learned from this dramatic scene that nature had just illustrated? I thought about what the Bible has to say pertaining to wolves, and I also thought about the community of deer. I have not heard of too many cases where wolves have actually attacked humans, but I have seen what they can do to a full-grown moose. It is a sickening thing to watch as ravenous wolves surround the moose, and nature follows its course to completion. The moose is able to fend off the wolves that charge from the front, but he has no defense against the wolves that lash at his hind legs. The wolves dart in biting and slashing at the moose's hind quarters until the hamstrings are severed and the moose collapses. Then, the frenzied wolves go for the soft under-belly and the throat. The chances of a moose's survival if attacked while alone are not good. However, if there is more than one moose, they become a formidable team, literally covering each other's backs. It is always the sick or wounded that seem to offer the best opportunity for an easy kill. They lag behind the rest of the group, or eventually become separated all together. Predators, such as the wolves lay in wait, watching the herd to single out the very young, the old, the lame, and the sick animals. The wolves are always watching from beyond the safety of the herd for just the right opportunity to make a strike.

I have seen this law of nature taking place in the spiritual realm, not against deer, or moose, but against people, and especially those in the Christian Community. I have been the sickly one that strayed away from community, taking lightly the command in Scripture that we are, "not to forsake the assembling of ourselves together." The herd knows where to find good food. The herd offers protection and warmth. They stay together, and the members offer their strengths and gifts in a way that benefits the whole community. My mother and father have always recognized this truth and have passed along the importance that a community of believers holds for the individual's spiritual well being. The Church is not a building where believers go once, or twice a week to perform rituals of worship. The Church is a family united in Christ Jesus where each part made up of the people, form a body, a living organism that functions as a whole. We were taught that to separate ourselves from the Church would be as foolish as a finger or toe trying to sustain life detached from the body. It just cannot be done. God designed us this way for a specific reason so that we would learn to be dependent on Him and others. We are only to separate from the community for short times to rest from our service, or for one-on-one alone time with the Lord for special attention and care, similar to when a finger has been broken and it must receive special attention before it can be returned to effective service.

The deer, the wolves, and even my fire that is now blazing in the stove, give credence to this law of community. The wolf hunts more effectively in community. The deer thrive in security and provision when they live in community. The fire cannot burn unless two or more sticks are joined together and set ablaze. I am beginning to see spiritual connections between the laws that govern our lives and those displayed in nature. The one mirrors the other if we are able to see beyond the limited reality we are used to. In Him, we really do live and move and have our being, and we are never living completely on our own, even if we avoid God and everyone else in our sphere of relationships. He is our vine, and we are the branches. We get our life from him, and if we want life from the vine then we must get it in close proximity to the other branches. Sorry, for you folks that are not very social, there are no lone twigs on a tree unless it is dying.

I used to think about the poor, solitary bucks roaming out in the forests on dark, cold nights. Now, my views have changed on the matter as I begin to understand more about the social characteristics of the deer species. The does, fawns, and even the younger bucks dwell in community through out the year. It is only during the mating season that the most selfish characteristics of the male deer can be witnessed in relationship to the rest of the community of deer. The buck is driven by only one motivation during the mating season and that is his compulsion to breed. The buck is fiercely independent and selfish. One or two does are not enough. He wants the whole territory and every doe within his territory. His drive to mate compels him back into community for a short time so that he can satisfy his needs. Once the mating season is completed, when the does are impregnated and discontinue their estrous cycle, the dominant buck resumes his separated life style. He leaves the responsibility of rearing the next generation of his offspring to the does, and the rest of the deer community. I suppose this is a natural instinct for the deer community, but being a "big buck" is not all it is cracked up to be, with all the long, lonely nights and the struggles to survive the many challenges in nature alone.

As in nature, so it is in the human community. Being a single, solitary "buck" is a lonely and dangerous way of life. I enjoy the time in solitude to meet with the Lord, because sometimes I am like the broken finger, or sometimes I need to rest and replenish my inner resources. Nevertheless, that is only one side of my physical and spiritual life. I am healed and nourished so that I may go and do the same. Life without purpose and participation is void of vitality. Others need me, and I need them. The wolves are out there whether or not we can see them, or hear them. It is never a good idea to stray too far from the herd, or we might get singled out and become an easy meal.

God designed us to be a part of his "herd." In His community we find security, provision, accountability, love, warmth, and fellowship. Outside of that community that He has provided for us we are just like the lonely buck, and the scary thing is that the hunting season never ends.

Chapter Eight

~The Ice Storm: Discoveries in the Stillness~

"Have you entered the storehouses of the snow or seen the
storehouses of the hail..."
~ Job 38:22

I awakened in the middle of the night to the sounds of sleet
tapping on my window. I lay there in the darkness for
quite some time, listening to other peculiar noises beyond
the sounds that first disturbed my sleep. It was ghostly, and
hauntingly eerie; like a woman wailing or a cat howling in
the distance. I did not realize what it was until the dawn
came and illuminated what had been happening during the
overnight hours. The forest was sparkling white, but not from

snow. Freezing rain had come during the night, and now the trees were cocooned in thick layers of ice. The wailing and moaning I had heard was not from cats or distraught women, but from sagging limbs that were bent under a heavy, icy load. Ice storms are the most inconspicuous of storms and yet they wreak incredible destruction in the end. These storms break the tops off even the largest of stately trees that have withstood the winds of violent gales, fiery bolts of lightning, and even occasional forest fires that have claimed many surrounding trees. On sunny days, the strong, giant boughs of the pine trees reach out to collect life-giving rays of sunshine that fall upon the woodlands, but during an ice storm, the sturdy outstretched beams of these great trees become their downfall. The forest is not a safe place to be during such an ice storm, not even in a well-built cabin, as we were to learn later in the day.

I was not sure what kind of work we would be doing during the ice storm. All of our lumber was encased in a solid block of ice, and venturing outside under the limbs of birch and pine proved to be quite unsettling as great limbs would suddenly missile down from the sky; like falling chandeliers in the old movies. Tinkling ice crystals would shower the ground as an early warning just before the dangerous, spiked limbs would pummel the ground. Despite the icy demolition outside, we met at the breakfast table to discuss the plans for the day. A hot meal of fried potatoes, scrambled eggs, sausage links, and blueberry bagels took the chill out of the morning. We decided that we should make our phone calls, and do anything else that might require electric power, or phone lines before the real damage of the storm could cut us off from the outside world. We knew our wives would see the news reports, and wonder about our safety. My brother was just starting to build a fire in the Ben Franklin stove when a thundering concussion interrupted the temporary silence. The transformer by the road had exploded when the connecting power lines could no longer endure the weight of the ice. What had been semi-quiet became absolute silence when the refrigerator compressor, ceiling fans, and electric space heaters ceased operation. So much for making any progress on the renovation project today, but all was not lost. We had managed to brew a pot of coffee in just the nick of time. It is amazing how peaceful it is when the power source is suddenly disrupted. We had just leaned back in our chairs to enjoy the coffee and the unplanned holiday, when- WHAM! The whole peninsula seemed to leap in the air. My brother and I both threw our coffee cups in the air and jumped from our chairs. Dust and cobwebs from the attic drifted down from the ceiling, and we both ran for the door. We could not see from the doorway what had just happened. So, we crept cautiously around the side of the cabin to have a look. An enormous limb had broken off from the giant pine tree that hovers over the cabin, and then another loud- CRACK! A birch tree snapped and thudded to the ground just a few feet away. We decided it was no longer safe to remain in the cabin, not with the huge pine tree overhead falling to pieces. If the whole tree toppled, it would flatten the cabin like a child stepping on a flimsy, toy house made of Popsicle sticks. We would have to leave the remodeling site, and spend the remainder of the day riding out the storm in the main lodge, where there was no danger from falling trees.

I quickly boxed up some food and supplies that we would need. There was no way of knowing how long it would be before we would be able to make it out to the main road, or when utility workers could get down to us. We checked to make sure all the power chords were unplugged and ensured that all the faucets were turned off. I practically skated with my box of goods down to the lodge. I had never seen an ice storm deposit such a thick glaze on everything. The ice was nearly an inch and a half thick on every exposed surface. I put the foodstuffs away and grabbed the little wagon to stock up on our wood supply. The lodge would quickly grow cold with no power for the main boiler.

The tarp covering the woodpile was as stiff as a sheet of plywood when I lifted it off to uncover the dry wood. Again, a falling limb landed just a few feet away from me. I decided that some haste would be a healthy thing. Then, I thought about our vehicles. Given the right trajectory, some of the leaning birch trees could do some serious damage if they toppled the wrong way. I would need to chip away some of the ice on the car doors and get the vehicles moved into the clearing. For a day that we had decided not to work, it sure seemed like there was a lot of work that needed to be done. After I moved the cars I resumed working on our wood supply. Once all of the emergency details were taken care of we could relax in the safety and warmth of the big lodge.

I put a pot of stew on the gas stove to boil and then set about starting a roaring fire in the giant fireplace. We toasted bread over a gas burner on the stove and lathered it with creamy butter. Wow! That stew was good, and it was comforting to be safe inside the sturdy lodge while the storm was slowly demolishing the outside world. The fire was warm and our stomachs were content. I went to get my guitar and sing a few songs while the setting of the sun hid the destruction from our view. My brother and my niece relaxed on the couches, curling up under the warm, fur throws. We idled away a couple of hours, talking and singing, and the whole scene looked like something from a Norman Rockwell Christmas card.

Sometimes God brings storms like these to make us slow down and appreciate the things that really matter in life. There is no guilt about missing work that should be getting done, because the electrical power is out. Isn't it sad that many times, we humans will not slow down until the power is completely out? In this case I am talking about the electricity, but I am also thinking about illness, or maybe down time that the loss of a job might cause. We think to ourselves, "What am I going to do? How am I going to earn a paycheck?" The Lord says, "Be still and know that I am God."

He is the God that brings ice storms. He is the God that sometimes touches us in a way that makes us realize our weakness. He is the God that feeds the sparrows, and tells us we are far more valuable than they. Oh, ye of little faith. I have heard it said that, "busyness is not of the Devil, it is the Devil." That is true, you know?

Sometimes God sends a storm that brings everything crashing down around us so that He can have our undivided attention. Take that time to enjoy the rest. Instead of looking for something to do, just rest and take a good look at what is really important in life– relationships. Relationships are the only thing you can take with you into the next life. So, the next time you find yourself waiting for a storm to pass you should ask God, "What do you want me to learn from this experience? Why did you put my project on ice?" Look around. Is there anyone you have been neglecting who needs a little more of your time? Could it be that God has put a freeze on all your busyness so that you can warm up to Him? Have all your "good activities" distracted you from that "better activity" of resting at His feet? Do not wiggle and fidget when your busyness gets put on hold. Take the time to refocus on what is really important, our relationship with God and with those precious people He has put in our lives. Do not worry, the ice will melt, the power will be restored, and you will return to productivity. Remember, that there is a season for everything, including some down time. I have found it to be true that it is during the periods of waiting, and ceasing our activity that some of the greatest work is being done.

Chapter Nine

~Deep Roots~

"That person is like a tree planted by streams of water, which yields its fruit in season and whose leaf does not wither—whatever they do prospers."
~ Psalm 1:3

I am always telling my family that I was born about a hundred and fifty years too late. I do not like what I see going on in our country today. The resources are getting pretty short, and unfortunately the people that have the most resources probably do not need them so much. There is an imbalanced, faulty system when it comes to the distribution of resources. The things we value the most in our country probably would not have been worth much one hundred and fifty years ago.

A baseball pitcher in the major leagues is said to have a "twenty million dollar arm", and yet the surgeon who knows how to repair that arm will probably never come close to making as much as that baseball player in comparison to his hourly investment of time. A master composer spends years studying music theory and composition, and he or she may labor for months over a particular piece of music that is so beautiful to the ears that even the angels in Heaven rejoice when it is played for the first time. But, the composer's reward for all his efforts may be menial in comparison to what some kid in a garage band receives after he sends in a digitally processed, computer enhanced track that he threw together in an afternoon. Meanwhile, the gifted composer fades into obscurity and survives marginally, teaching others the sacred art of music in a local community college, but is never fully appreciated for his expertise. The surgeon is paid well, but the training costs, the risks, and the amount of time involved in building his practice may cost him dearly before he sees a return on his investment; somewhere about the mid point of his career. That is, if he is fortunate.

Did I mention that I feel like I was born a hundred and fifty years too late? It is not that I hate technology. I use and enjoy various gadgets that make my life easier and more entertaining. Nevertheless, I am very cautious, because I think technology is robbing us of the struggles that teach us how to adapt to our environment and become more resourceful, independent, and capable people.

The irony is that environmental scientists and associated analysts say that in a decade or two (should the Lord tarry His coming) the survival of humankind will depend largely on how quickly we can make the transition back to the basics. They are saying that we will be anything but a global economy. Limited fuel sources and modes of transportation will necessitate small communities where people live, work, and travel in a very small radius. Everyone will have a trade that directly relates to the survival of the small community. Once again, the farmer and the country doctor will be a huge asset to the community and no one will be clamoring for the latest basketball shoes, they will get on a list to have the local cobbler come and make their shoes while he eats dinner at their table and sleeps under their roof— credit cards not accepted; wagon wheels or a side of beef, maybe.

Luxury cars will probably be melted down to make plows and garden tools, and we will return to true horsepower. I am pretty fond of that notion. I can relate to talking to your horses and praising them for their efforts. I have never understood why guys talk to their car like it was a spouse, or a best friend. I am all for doctors and ministers being once again elevated to a position worthy of someone who cares for the well being of body and soul. I am all for seeing the burden of welfare put back into the hands of the family and church. Instead of passing out green treasury checks, I look forward to seeing green gardens, green thumbs, and the blessing of fellowship that results from families working together for the common good.

We admire the Amish people for their simple way of living, but not too many of us would exchange our lives of comfort for their sweat. I say we have missed the big picture entirely. We leave our families to go off to work so we can drive fancy cars and own fancy homes while our children sit in their rooms watching television and playing video games. Once the kids get their driver's license we may never see them again on a regular basis until they retire, if we are still alive by then. In the Amish home, bedrooms were built with the intention of providing a place to sleep and get dressed. Dark rooms are boring, so the living room by the fireplace is where the light, warmth, and activity can be found. Horses do not have headlights, so they get returned to the barn before dark. I have never heard of two Amish kids dying in a head on collision between two horses. Nor, have I heard of too many drinking and driving infractions by those that travel by horse and buggy. The crazy thing is that the Amish keep themselves busy and they do not seem to have many cases of "emerging adulthood." They are men and women who have learned life skills by the time they are ready to wed. Call me old fashioned, but I think the simple living Amish people are the ones who are ahead of the times, because they already know how to live self sufficiently and maintain sustainable environs. I could really drag this illustration out, but I do not think I need to.

There are dangers when we substitute video games, televisions, and gadgets for human interaction. The Scriptures say that people create idols that have eyes, mouths, and ears, but they do not really see, speak, or hear and those that worship these idols become like them. Have you noticed the lack of sincere gratitude these days? The toys get bigger and more expensive with each passing year. The games and graphics are incredible and, oh yes, very stimulating. Even grown men and women are caught in this spiral of the senses. Technology has robbed us of one of life's greatest gifts— contentment. Not in things, or abundance of them, but contentment, only found in close relationships with God, friends, and the family members we love. It is like an "Alexander the Great/Solomon syndrome," by mid-life we stand there looking at everything, and we either weep, because "there are no more worlds to conquer", or else we shake our heads thinking, "Vanity, all is vanity."

Do not get me wrong, not all pleasure or excitement is wrong, but it must be seasoned and balanced with a certain amount of struggle and even some suffering. The truly mature are those who have faced adversity in life and as a result have the inner strength to face times of suffering when they come.

I am thinking about last week's ice storm. I believe the Lord taught me something in the aftermath of the ice storm about the value of struggles. Many times He speaks clearly to me through lessons in nature. Following the ice storm, I looked around the property, noticing all of the fallen trees, and those that were still standing. I noticed that in the case of the trees that were still standing, their survival had nothing to do with their visible characteristics; such as how big they were around the base, or how thick their limbs were, or how much vitality they seemed to have. To be honest, some of them looked like a small gust of wind could have toppled them. I did notice that some of the greenest and most healthy looking trees were the ones that were snapped in two, or easily toppled, almost as if there were no great deal of force involved in pulling them down. They were snapped in two because they were top heavy. They had become too heavy at the top due to quick growth shoots, but had not had sufficient time to develop deep enough roots to anchor them. There were trees that were so dead that you could almost see daylight through the holes in their trunks, but they were stripped of the heavy limbs during past storms and thus able to stand the heavy coats of ice in this recent storm. The trees in the fertile bowl had the worst damage. Years of silt deposits, and ample water had pampered these trees. Their roots were very shallow and they were extremely top heavy. Before they toppled over they looked like a bunch of flimsy cattails bowed over by all the weight, their trunks green and spongy from too much hydration. Then, there were the champions of my illustration, straight and true, with sturdy roots to anchor them. These trees seemed to be in the worst possible places, frequently wedged between the cracks in the rocks on the hillside; roots uncovered by the erosion of wind and water; exposed to the elements, but having big and deep roots, nonetheless. The tallest trees were the ones atop the rocky hillside where the strongest winds have blown for decades, and their position in life had kept them out of reach of the water soaked basin below. These trees have stood the tests of time, and each year they have grown stronger from the deprivations of dry, rocky soil— growing slowly, but sure and strong. Then, when nature's severest tests have come along, such as last week's ice storm, they stand with a certain sense of quiet grace as they overlook the destruction down in the wet, fertile valley below.

I see a connection between the trees and the verse in Proverbs 13:24 that says, *"Whoever spares the rod hates his son, but he who loves him is diligent to discipline him."* A life of plenty and favorable circumstances is not as beneficial in the long run as we would think. Consider a butterfly as she struggles out of a cocoon before she can take flight. The road less traveled by the Amish People is a road that is scoffed at by the modern, high-tech world, but that high-tech world is the same multitude choosing the easy way that Jesus speaks of when He said, "Enter through the narrow gate. For wide is the gate and broad is the road that leads to destruction, and many enter through it" (Matthew 7:13). It is easy to be deceived when you think the road is safe because so many people are on it. I will give you a hint: you probably will not find the narrow way using a modern GPS, but you might find it through an ancient "GPS"- Grief, Pain, and Suffering. Remember that Jesus promised the abundant life to those who would follow Him, but He also promised that in this life there would be many trials and times of suffering. That may sound like a contradiction, but it is not if you understand the connection between present suffering and future glory. Present suffering prepares us for future glory.

If today you find yourself in dry, rocky soil, and it seems like this season in time is more about suffering and stagnation rather than joy, highlighted with quick spurts of growth, take courage and trust the wisdom of God. After the storms of adversity cease, you will be firmly rooted, standing tall on a hillside while those who have only known ease, become bowed and broken beyond hope of repair. Be content wherever you are planted in this stage of life, and then let your roots grow slowly, and deeply.

Chapter Ten

~Fortitude~

"In your unfailing love you will lead the people you have redeemed. In your strength you will guide them to your holy dwelling."
~ Exodus 15:13

The Spruce trees are dancing to welcome the arrival of spring, though we humans are unable to see that it is coming. The white caps on Lake Superior are cresting at about twelve feet. Winds are barreling in at sixty miles per hour. A gale is raging tonight, despite the starry skies above. The deck is glazed with ice from the spray of enormous waves that have been crashing on the rocks surrounding the peninsula where our sturdy lodge stands. The ground is shaking from the intensity of millions of gallons of surging water that pummels the shoreline every few seconds. The magnitude of the force generated by the wind surge humbles me even though my feet are stationed on solid ground. The very thought of being out on the open water on a night like this, sends icy chills down my spine.

I guess that is why I am so shocked to see the lights of a ship out in the violent darkness. I am amazed that any captain would risk his boat and crew trying to cross this deadly lake on such a night as this. The bottom of Lake Superior is strewn with broken ships and courageous men who dared to venture away from safe havens under these sorts of conditions, the most famous being the wreckage of the Edmund Fitzgerald. What is the impetus behind a ship and crew sailing against such contrary seas? What sustains a man's courage when he must steady himself on a deck that rolls like a moving hillside?

A night like this reminds me of a story in the book of Matthew. Jesus had just fed a multitude with impossibly small resources, and evidently His group of future world-shaking disciples had not made the connection. They were still struggling with unbelief, and at times indifferent to the people Jesus was serving. Jesus decided it was time for a little lesson. So, before He sent the crowds away, He sent His own disciples on a ride they would never forget. Jesus is sometimes seen as "The Gentle Shepherd", at other times "The Great Physician", but on this occasion He was the "Great Teacher".

Back in my football days, the coaches were implementing a new technique in strength training called "negative resistance." If your goal were to bench press 350 lbs, 400 lbs would be loaded on to the bar with the assistance of two spotters, one on each side. The spotters would lower the bar until your arms supported the full weight. You did not have to lift the weight off your chest; you simply had to suffer under the weight until your arms could no longer bear it without the aid of your helpers. The helpers, upon seeing the wobbling of your arms and the likelihood of coming collapse, would then help you lift the bar back on to the pegs. You were given a few minutes to rest and then the process was repeated until every bit of strength had been drained from your arms. Each training day, the weight would be increased by twenty pounds. After the negative resistance-training period, we were granted a few days of rest before we attempted the goal weight of our choosing. When the spotters lowered the goal weight on to our hands we were amazed at how light the load seemed to be. Most of us were able to not only lift that previously impossible weight, but also to lift it three to five times in repetition. What had seemed like an impossible goal was easily attainable, because we had briefly borne the weight of a heavier burden with the intermittent assistance of our helpers. When it came time for us to attempt the impossible on our own, our confidence had grown so much that we believed we could actually do it. Once the mind was convinced, the muscles (flesh) followed suit. Does that not sound like the makings of a possible sermon?

When you hear the word, "comfort" what do you normally think? If you are like most people, you think of a big, fat, overstuffed recliner, fuzzy slippers, or a well-worn fleece sweatshirt. In actuality, the word "comfort" at the root means to fortify, or to come and strengthen. Well, in Jesus' own way, He was about to comfort His disciples by sending them out in a boat, not down to the nearest safe harbor, but

He instructs them to cross over the lake to the other side. About half way across the lake, He sends a little comfort the disciple's way. No, not Ben & Jerry's ice cream, or Columbia parkas, but contrary seas like the ones I have been marveling at tonight. Jesus brewed up a nice one just to teach the boys a little about who He is, just in case they are still slow in coming to conclusions. It is interesting to note that they were in the middle of their voyage when the storm confronted them. I suppose they could have put up their sails and let the storm carry them back to shore. Nevertheless, I am sure they talked among themselves and decided that Jesus must have had a precise reason He wanted them to meet Him at the appointed location. Maybe they thought that He would need their assistance at the next gathering, and would be disappointed if they did not obey His instructions. So, they endured, doing what they knew was His bidding, even though it meant risking their lives, and the boat. They fought against the storm all night until they were probably beyond fatigue, and losing hope that they would ever overcome the opposing wind and waves to make it to their appointed destination.

Have you ever noticed that Jesus is never in a rush, but he is always on time? Just when all other options are no longer options, when fatigue has been elevated to despair and panic, and when all hope is gone, or as the Scripture tells us, "about the third watch of the night", just before dawn, when the night has reached its darkest point, Jesus comes to them walking on the stormy sea. They thought He was a ghost. Hey, we have all been there, thinking to our selves, "How could this situation possibly get any worse?" They were probably thinking, "Only the Devil would be out, and about during a storm like this. Bummer, dudes! There he is now."

Well, that is what happens sometimes when we are being put to the test, and the test lingers a little longer than we had expected. I am sure we have all been in the disciple's boat and thought, "It is just no use and it is way too late for God to do anything in this mess I am in now. The forces of darkness are after us and we had better row even harder now, or our ship is sunk for sure."

But, oh how wonderful to be in that hopeless situation, and like the disciples, hear His voice saying, "Fear not, it is I." How astonished they must have been. I can just see those exhausted, soaked to the skin, half-drowned disciples waving their hands in the air, and crying out with unspeakable joy. It is the same for us when He brings peace to us in our storms. Now, get this: Jesus gets into the boat, and suddenly, they were where they were going. The training session is over; the turmoil, confusion, and panic disappear in the early morning light. They arrive at the destination that only a few minutes before, none of them had believed they would reach.

A portion of courage comes from the realization that God is in control of the intensity, and the duration of life's storms. The other part of courage comes from the belief that the Sender of the storm will also be present through it. We are not called to conquer the storms, or make it through on our own; we are only required to endure the storms with faith. There is a physical side to courage, but there is also a virtue called fortitude, which means perseverance and endurance. We persevere by leaning on the One who has the strength to carry us through, and that is where the true comfort is found. Are you seeing Jesus in your storm, or just a ghost trying to sink your boat? Listen for that still, small voice that can be heard despite the crashing waves all around you. Hear that whisper, "Fear not, it is I." Celebrate His arrival in your crisis, and by all means invite Him into your boat if you have not already done so.

One of my favorite preachers, Carter Conlon, was using an illustration in one of his messages. I will share with you the unique insight that God gave him. Carter and his wife Teresa were vacationing on the New England Coast. One day a real gale was unleashing its furry with enormous white caps and thundering waves. The storm was so violent, he could barely see through the torrent, and to his amazement, out in the middle of the bay, bobbed a little duck, riding high on the crested waves. Though the powerful waves were raging toward the shore, the little duck rode up and over the enormous swells as she paddled against the surge. Even the powerful pull of the ocean was not hindering the little duck from reaching her intended destination. Carter said that the Lord taught him a powerful lesson with what he had seen. The storm was not a challenge for that little duck; she was just doing what God designed her to do; swim against the mighty forces of the sea.

We should appreciate the way God designed us; each with our own unique characteristics, like the little duck. When we are carrying out our unique purpose, it is not a burden. We should not "duck" our heads, and allow the surge to sweep us away. We should take courage in the fact that God has prepared us for just this circumstance and this circumstance just for us. The storms are not meant to destroy us, but to strengthen us, and help us function the way God intended. We put our trust in the God who designed us, and will give us every provision for every purpose He has called us to. The storms of life inevitably will come, they are guaranteed to come our way, but through each storm you can be confident that our present suffering is preparing for us, what the Apostle Paul describes as, "an eternal weight of glory." So, take your eyes off of the waves, and quit looking for ghosts. Instead, close your eyes and listen with your heart for that still, small voice of Jesus, "Fear not, it is I."

Chapter Eleven

~Persevering~

"For our light and momentary troubles are achieving for us an eternal glory that far outweighs them all."
~ 2 Corinthians 4:17

I have heard it said that what is accomplished during the waiting is often more important than what we are waiting for. Inevitably, at some point in life we will find ourselves waiting for something that will test us beyond our capacity to cling to hope, and despite our strong resolve, unbelief comes drifting in like a dark, mysterious fog. God seems to have left us scratching our heads, as the circumstances do not turn out like we had expected. At the onset we may have thought to ourselves, "I have faced testing and trials before, and God will surely hear my prayer and resolve this situation just as He has done in the past, maybe not today, this week, or even in the months to come, but I will pull up my bootstraps and wait patiently until the day He moves on my behalf, in due time." The crisis comes when our "due time" is not the equivalent of God's "due time." Hopes and dreams of deliverance seem to fade away until all that remains is our dejection and despair. Why is this so? If God is a loving father, why does He so often place some of His most earnest children in the crucible of waiting, when it seems that some of His, less devoted fledglings seem to get ready answers to their prayers? Prolonged periods of waiting, and unanswered prayers can foster dark questions in the heart of a downcast believer, even to the point of questioning the validity of their position in Christ. I believe, and others have given assent to the same notion, that we should never compare the circumstances of our own walk with God, to that of another believer's walk with God. Some believers may seem very mature in their faith, when in fact they are only babes in Christ. It seems that sometimes, God caters to the whims of new believers by keeping their milk bottles full, and by pampering their tender emotions with ready affirmations. Nevertheless, as He recognizes spiritual growth and maturity in new believers, He begins to wean them to more solid fare. He is forever coaxing them to the next level. Some are content to stay as "babes", but they will never discover the joy and strength that comes from a solid faith that is anchored in the goodness of God, despite contrary circumstances. A "babe" must be constantly cared for, and has little usefulness in advancing the kingdom of God. Furthermore, they do not compound as many eternal rewards as the mature believer who is led and filled by the Holy Spirit on a daily basis. The "babe" wants to coast through life with training wheels to keep him steady.

It is a spiritual hunger and thirst for the greater mysteries of God and deeper spiritual intimacy that forces the "babe" to transition from training wheels, and begin to cry out to God for more. God answers this cry of the heart, but often not in the way we would expect. It is like the guy who prays, "God please give me patience, and by the way I would like it now." I think of Joseph in the Genesis account, where God tested him in a way that seemed beyond human endurance. God transformed Joseph from a pampered, spoiled teenager into a wise ruler who saved the lives of millions of people when famine hit the land.

It is hard to envision the end results of our suffering, and we do not always understand the path on which God sometimes places us that will eventually lead to incredible blessings. I have seen this principle revealed in the processes of nature. This rugged, Northern Wilderness where I reside is full of breathtaking beauty, but it is also a land of severity. Before the beauty is revealed, there is a prolonged period of death and silence. The previous season's beauty dies and gives way to months of deep snow, ice, and temperatures that can average twenty below zero in the winter.

I understand now, why Paul says that all of creation groans for release and restoration. I like to think of that coming day as perpetual springtime, when the flowers continually bloom, the bass are always biting, and there is no traumatic swing in the climate. As I look around the grounds, it appears that the death grip of winter is losing its hold. The trees are budding now, despite nighttime temperatures that still dip below freezing. A trip to the ridge yesterday revealed that the deer herd has survived the long winter though there are not as many of them congregating up in the bowl. I prefer to think that the missing ones have moved on to greener, sunnier hillsides to feast and prepare to give birth to their young, which is the case for many of them. Nevertheless, I will also be realistic and acknowledge the fact that many of the deer that I have watched from day to day probably did not survive the periods of extreme cold and scarcity of forage. The scarcity of forage is what drove many of them down into the resort despite their natural fear of human proximity.

I have been especially fond of the little yearling buck that has been frequenting the hillside every day to nibble on the remaining raspberry bushes. He disappeared in February when the blizzards ferociously scoured the hillsides, and temperatures dropped to minus thirty-two degrees. I do not know how any of the forest animals like the deer can survive such extremes with so little shelter and provision. I noticed a parallel to the illustration of "babes" transitioning from training wheels, when in autumn the temperatures start to slowly fall, and the deer's winter coat thickens in preparation for the deep freeze to come. I have noticed that the fur and the hide of Northern deer are much denser than their Southern relatives. Maybe the reason the Northern deer stay so hearty is that they never get to experience any prolonged seasons of comfort and plenty. They only seem to experience a short period of respite during the three months of true summer, and it is at this time of the year that they quickly regain strength and body mass. They are always prepared for the worst, and nature seems to constantly test their readiness.

Recently, I read a story about a woman who was a long-distance swimmer, and in the story, she was attempting the longest swim of her career. On the day that she was to make her attempt, the weather had turned foul. A heavy fog and contrary waves came against her as she struggled to cover the distance. She gave it her best effort, but gave up when she could no longer find the strength to continue. Men in the guide boats had to pull her from the water and ferry her to land. She was nearly heartbroken to find that she had given up only a short distance from the shore. Later, she told reporters that if there would not have been such a heavy fog, and if only she could have seen what lay ahead of her, she would have had the courage to continue. It was the uncertainty that had stolen her strength to endure.

Sometimes, life can be like that when we feel like we have been swimming against the opposition for far too long, and it appears that there is no end in sight. We carry a heavy burden for weeks and those weeks can stretch into months until we eventually lose hope that the fog will ever lift, and we will return to some semblance of stability. We throw in the towel, never knowing how close we were to the long awaited shore. It has been said that the darkest hour is just before the dawn. There are times when we simply cannot lose faith in God. Too many people are watching our faith in the crucible, and if we go down, they go down as well. There have been many times that I would have preferred to throw in the towel on this renovation project. The rewards have not appeared to be worth the sacrifices being made. The living and travel expenses seem to have taken a pretty big chunk out of the profits, but I have found that the true rewards have nothing to do with money.

On one occasion, Jesus' disciples asked Him where He had found food, and He told them that He had food that they knew nothing about; His food was to do the will of His Father. You can take the word, "food" out of the sentence and replace it with many things— joy, peace, profit, security, strength, sense of purpose, etc. A great salary does not constitute a great job if it robs you of any thing I just listed. There are seasons of life when it seems that we are like the deer left out in the extreme elements with little provision and shelter. It is during these times that we must trust, more than any other time, in the goodness of God, knowing that He sees the true needs we have before we even ask Him. As the trials press us in nearer to the shelter of his arms, we will begin to see that He does prepare a table for us in the presence of our enemies, whether the enemies take the form of sickness, persecution, financial trouble, depression, or doubts. Our Lord has promised that He would not abandon us as orphans, but that He would come to us. If there were no trouble, there would be no need for the promised Comforter. I would not trade anything for the experiences of His presence that I have found in the worst trials of my life. We are not called to persevere through the storms of life on our own; we are called to wait upon the Lord, taking shelter in Him until He lifts us in His "due time." We will emerge from these seasons of waiting stronger in our faith, and changed in our hearts. The flowers will smell sweeter and the days of spring will offer a glimpse of how it will one day be for all of eternity. We will agree with Paul when he says that the suffering that we experience now is only "light and momentary." Can this be true in every circumstance? Most of my trials, and the suffering I have witnessed other's experience, could hardly be called, "light and momentary," but if you view the suffering and trials on the timeline of eternity, and consider the magnitude of the dividends we will some day receive for our suffering, then yes, our sufferings now will not even seem worth mentioning.

The pain of waiting sometimes seems intolerable, but it is usually negligible in contrast to the value of what is being birthed. The book of Isaiah has a passage that illustrates this point and it reads as follows, "Do I bring to the moment of birth and not give delivery?" says the LORD. "Do I close up the womb when I bring to delivery?" says your God" (Isaiah 66:9). If you are waiting and longing for something to be birthed in you, the chances are good that God initiated that longing, and He intends to finish what He has begun.

Chapter Twelve

~Restored~

"The poor and needy search for water, but there is none; their tongues are parched with thirst. But I the LORD will answer them; I, the God of Israel, will not forsake them. I will make rivers flow on barren heights, and springs within the valleys. I will turn the desert into pools of water, and the parched ground into springs."
~ Isaiah 41: 17,18

We are beginning to see a light at the end of the tunnel, and we are almost sure it is not a train. It is amazing how quickly renovation can take place after all of the demolition, and preliminary alterations have been made. My brother and I both said that we hope we never have to do renovation work again. There is so much extra work involved in remodeling compared to new construction. Nevertheless, as I look around at what we have accomplished, I realize that there would have been no other way to recapture the original charm and beauty that this nostalgic retreat once had. It probably would have been much quicker and easier to bulldoze the old structures into the clearing and set them ablaze so that we could start with fresh foundations and new materials. The problem exists in the fact that new buildings would not fit in with the history of this place. Sometimes there is greater potential value in working with what already exists; no matter what shape it is in. The good doctor that owns this resort has an eye for such treasures, and is not willing that "anything" should perish, much to our chagrin at certain times. He did not want this place to be like one of the many corporate ventures that seem to be popping up so quickly, commercializing this pristine wilderness region. He wanted to restore more than just the walls of the broken down buildings. He was hoping to recapture the sentiment of a bygone era, when families used to come and find rest by sidestepping all of the trappings of modern conveniences, and the distractions that come with them. The original buildings represent a golden age that has long since been trampled underfoot and forgotten. It was a time when all the work was done by hand, when the work represented more than just a paycheck, and a man's finished craft was a reflection of who he was as a person.

We made a special discovery a few weeks ago while we were rummaging through the old pole barn at the top of the hill. We found the original advertising flyers for the resort, which had been printed back in the 1930's. I had originally hoped to include some of the pictures from the flyer alongside some of the present photographs, but the image quality was too bad. The pictures in the flyer were taken from the south end of the property, facing the rear of the cabin. In the flyer there is a noticeable clump of three birch trees in the center of the property. If you could see the flyer and the present photographs, you would agree that the three birch trees in the clump are the same ones standing there today, nearly eighty years later. Those three birch trees have special significance to me. They represent time, continuity, and stability. I think of how many storms they have weathered. How they have always been there during the years since the cabin was first built. They are like a trio of protective guardians, following close behind. They have been a part of the surroundings, though not in the forefront of the cabin's history and circle of activity. It is almost as if they have been standing there, silently watching the life of the cabin, from its early days and vigorous years of service, through the long years of neglect, and even now as the tired, old cabin has been restored and made ready to serve again. Perhaps, this was one of the most meaningful things the Lord has shown me during my time here as I have slowly discovered that the restoration work we have been doing has mirrored a deeper work he has wrought in me and in those around me.

In my younger years, I was like the old cabin after it was first built— fresh, clean, sturdy, and productive. People would frequently come and go through the doors of my life. The times were exciting and fast paced, but there was no real continuity, there were no true, enduring relationships. Life was about quick turnover, and rushing to produce a better future for myself, never wondering what had happened to the people who came and went. For a while I believed that I was making great headway climbing the ladder of success, and compiling the rewards of my pursuits. However, like the old cabin, the fast paced turnover, and drive to produce without taking time for rest and repair, had left me broken down on the exterior, dirty and diseased on the interior. People still came and went, but they no longer saw the inviting appearance which was once there, but had slowly faded over time. Some would pass by for a brief look, but after seeing what was inside, they just kept going. And then, after a while, no one came through my doors at all. There was nothing inviting to see, and since I was no longer productive, I was no longer of any value to anyone. For years, I stood in the darkness, broken and forgotten, just like the old cabin. Nevertheless, I still had my own trio of guardians that stood nearby, quietly watching in the shadows of my ruin. Then, one day the Doctor arrived and saw that there was still some potential, and he developed a vision of restoration. At certain times none of it made sense as he moved a lot of junk around the place, even adding to the already overflowing accumulation of debris. Nevertheless, once everything had been inventoried, he decided what would stay and what would have to go. Only the things that could be reused in the renovation were saved, and the rotted, clutter some materials were hauled away. The Doctor had hired several workers to undertake the project, and complete the vision he had for his neglected, rundown property. The first workers proved to be unfaithful to the task, so he hired more, but they cut corners and he had to let them go, too. Finally, he enlisted the help of a worker that would give himself to the task until it was completed. There have been arguments and disagreements on how the work was to be done, but despite the obstacles, the work continues and the restoration is coming along nicely. I suppose by now you are wondering whether I am talking about myself, or the cabin. Well, both. If you understood what I was alluding to, you might recall times where certain circumstances paralleled what was transpiring in your own heart. It is a familiar feeling as if you have trod that path before.

When I was a young man, I always thought that someday God would somehow appear to me in some kind of "burning bush," as He had appeared to Moses. I expected to hear an audible voice coming from some ethereal cloud in front of me that would tell me what to do with my life, who to marry, and how things would turn out for me if I continued the journey. I kept straining my eyes forward and had failed to notice how evident God had been in my past, always leaving His divine finger prints here and there, and like the trio of trees, He had been hovering close behind me all the time. The Scripture says that we will hear an unknown (unrecognized) voice coming over our shoulder saying, "This is the way, walk ye in it." I do not think that "over our shoulder" is really where the voice is coming from. I think the admonition is for us to look back, to remember the former things. We are to recall the chapters of our lives, and when we do, we will plainly see how God has continually revealed himself through the circumstances of our lives. If we take a long hard look at the past we will come to a realization, just like the Prodigal Son in Luke's Gospel did, that we were bankrupt, hungry, dirty, and in danger. Restoration began when we saw the folly of going our own way, and realized how far we had wandered from home. The good news is that the very second we turned and started walking home; the Father had already started running to meet us, and He will restore everything of value that was lost in our wanderings. "Home" is that place of rest that God desires each of us to enter. As we spend time in His presence, restoration is set in motion in our lives. The more we are restored, the closer we will come to the abundant life that Jesus speaks of in John 10:10. Satan steals, kills, and destroys but Jesus makes all things new. He is the consummate "Restorer" and as He finishes His work in us, we come to discover what abundant life is all about.

Chapter Thirteen

~Living at Rest~

*"This is what the Sovereign LORD, the Holy One of Israel,
says: "In repentance and rest is your salvation, in quietness
and trust is your strength..."*
~ Isaiah 30:15

I was rather surprised recently, to find out that a musician, and man of God that I greatly respected, had become a recluse. This man used his incredible musical talent as a platform to spread the Gospel. His heavenly voice and prowess on the guitar strings would soften hearts so that the seeds of the gospel message could be planted. Perhaps, he discovered what I have discovered on the North Shore, and that is the presence of God when we separate ourselves from worldly distractions, and quiet ourselves before Him. The danger of becoming solely focused on this type of pursuit is that we can become spiritually indulgent and selfish. I am hoping that this man is only using this time to rest, and gather spiritual resources so that he can return to be of even greater service to the Kingdom than he was before.

Early on in this project, I believe that I would have liked to pitch my tent and make seclusion a way of life, but I realized that the reason I was given the opportunity to discover this fountain of renewal, was so that I could share my experiences with others. Though it has been nearly a year since I left the North Shore, I am still learning things from that experience.

One thing that I have learned is that location should not determine our state of rest. If we find that we can only come near to God in certain locations, we will be tempted to idolize the geography, and not the God who inhabits that place. Sometimes it is necessary to come away from humanity to encounter God's presence, but while we are there we should learn what elements were involved in that encounter. Those elements are the ones that we need to take with us wherever we go, incorporating them into our daily lives.

We have all heard the proverb, "the early bird gets the worm." Well, you will not find that anywhere in the Bible, but it does contain a measure of spiritual truth. We all have a tendency to be a "Martha," to the extent of laboring hard for the Lord and His work, but it is in that context that He told Martha, "Only one thing is needful." Mary had discovered that "One thing," sitting at Jesus' feet. We will find that all we need can be found there, too. I do not believe He meant that we are to lounge around in careless ease, but I believe that He was emphasizing the importance of setting our priorities aright. If we give the Lord first place with our time, seeking

Him and His wisdom first, before we rush into the day, we will discover that we have His wisdom to organize our time and make the best use of the hours we have been allotted each day. Time is our most valuable resource. If we do not honor God with our time, by putting Him first in the day, how can we expect Him to bless our endeavors? I used to think that it did not matter when you met with the Lord, as long as you did meet with Him daily. The problem with this thinking is that it is like reading the directions after you have already baked the cake and then realized that you forgot the eggs. The cake does not turn out too well if you try to add the eggs after it is baked. My wise friend, Dr. Shepson says, "The symphony tunes before the performance." I'm sure that you understand the principle.

There have been so many times that I have encountered situations in my day that God's Word had clearly addressed that morning in my reading. It was a concern that fell somewhere in the gray area, but the Word gave me added perspective, and helped me make a more precise decision about that matter.

At the present time, my academic study is focused on the sentence structure and form that the writers of the Scriptures used. Often, the writers would state the main point, and then use illustrations to add more emphasis. They would often use an antithesis, so that the reader would understand from a negative standpoint what the effect would be if certain admonitions were not followed. Psalms 63:1 may be such an antithesis, "O God, thou art my God; early will I seek thee: my soul thirsteth for thee, my flesh longeth for thee in a dry and thirsty land, where no water is". The psalmist says that he hungers for this time with God in such a way that he is like a man stranded in the desert with no food, or water. We can easily understand David's analogy and even agree with him, but even so, we run out the door each morning, forgetting that we are heading into the desert of a fallen world without any provision. Without this morning "manna" how can we expect to get very far if we are merely subsisting on last night's meal? I am not advocating a type of "time clock" spirituality where we force ourselves to put in time before the Lord. No, to see it as such, shows that we do not see the value of what is being offered. Jesus is our life, if we do not attach ourselves to Him daily, preferably before the cares of the world have captured our attention, our spiritual life will become anemic, and may eventually wither and die.

Over the past year, the Lord has been encouraging me to set aside the first hour of the day for Scripture reading and prayer. I almost need a sign on the door to remind myself each morning. I do not sit still very well. My mind is very project oriented, and the devil capitalizes on this weakness of mine. In order to consistently make this early morning meeting with the Lord happen, it requires focused planning the day before. It requires that I give Him the honor that He deserves. Putting Him first requires that I think about Him when I rise in the morning, throughout the day, and again as the day draws to a close. It is easy to get tempted by a last minute project the night before that will thwart the possibility of an early rendezvous with the Lord the next morning.

Why is it so hard for us humans to cease our activity and turn in for the night? Being a person that is driven is not an admirable character trait. If we are driven, we are slaves to an evil master. Such a master is one that seeks to drive us right into the ground. God wants us to get our proper rest so that we can fully function in His Kingdom purposes. Then, we will be alert enough to recognize His leading when He sends divine opportunities our way.

Jesus narrowed the necessities of life down to one thing. Less is better! So much of the time, we are in a frenzy trying to "seize the day;" we are always running and grasping for a myriad of experiences and "things". Things are to be used in this life to assist us, not control us. The more things we try to seize, the more they seize and divide our thinking and desires. When this happens we can never fully invest our hearts in any single purpose. When this is the case, even our best efforts tend to be halfhearted. I think that is why Jesus told us to seek first the kingdom of God, and His righteousness, and then, all these "things" would be added unto us. When our pursuits are pure, and wholly focused on God, things will not enslave our minds and activities. With keener focus, our endeavors will be much more fruitful.

We cannot serve God, and worldly pursuits. When we serve God whole heartedly, "things" stop controlling us and, like Paul, we become content in all situations whether we have very little, or great abundance. When the things of this world cease to be our driving motivation we can learn to "sit still" at the Master's feet, and it is there that we learn to rest. It is that "rest" that we are to strive to enter into.

Why does the Scripture say we must strive to enter that rest? That sounds like an oxymoron, doesn't it? The reason is that we must battle against an unholy drive to achieve and acquire those things that would distract us from the "one needful thing," finding God, and resting at His feet. The still, attentive posture before God is the only place we can

find life and be transformed into the image of His Son. The
Son is complete in every way. He lives at rest and His peace
that passes all understanding can be ours when we seek His
kingdom first above all other things.

When all of the senseless ambition and frenzy is laid to
rest, and we enter into the peace that is found in communion
with God, the natural desire is to go, and share this newfound
life and peace with others. We cannot share this life until we
have experienced it for ourselves. Like the disciples, we must
tarry until we are endued with power from Heaven. Why
did Jesus tell his disciples to wait? Because, the flesh profits
nothing! They would have been rushing out in their own
steam and the results would have been disastrous. God's
purposes must be accomplished with God's resources. Apart
from Him, we have nothing and we can do NOTHING!

There was a time in my life when I was working really
hard to please God with my life and my service. It seemed
like the greater my effort the more my failure. I could not
understand why God was not blessing my devotion, and He
seemed so distant. I started to study the works of Charles
H. Spurgeon as he expounded on the book of Romans. I
had fallen back into a legalistic, "Old Covenant" mindset. I
started to read, and reread Romans again, meditating on what
the Holy Spirit was saying. I discovered that religious fervor,
and service compelled by duty only, amounts to nothing
more than dead works. Everything we are trying to earn by
our duty and goodness actually places us under God's wrath.
I began to see why it is so hard for performance oriented
humans to accept grace. We have grown up so brainwashed
that we must earn everything that represents any value. We
do not need, and do not want any charity. Charity makes

us look incapable and needy. Nevertheless, it is only in that beggarly state that we can receive anything from God. Any motive of performance, undermines the magnitude of God's grace, and magnifies our stinking pride.

We must first see how bankrupt we are spiritually; before we can ever be in a position to receive the blessings He has in store for us. Pride is the greatest blocker of God's grace. The grace of God can only flow down to the lowly of heart? down to the sinner who has bowed at His feet.

Jesus never hurried, but neither did He ever waste any time. We have much to learn from His example. By nature I am a checklist person. For some reason, I have to have all of my tasks charted so that I can prioritize my activities and mark them off upon completion. The problem with this approach is that sometimes the variables can change from day to day. Some tasks that probably should receive less attention somehow wind up at the top of the list, and the truly urgent items somehow seem to get lost in the shuffle. Some people will not have anything to do with a checklist, because checklists destroy spontaneity. Some folks have such detailed lists that they can account for every five minute block of time in their day. I am still trying to decide what a comfortable fit is for me. Everyone should have some form of record to keep track of his or her daily responsibilities, but I have seen this either overdone, or painfully neglected. I am finding that "less" really is better. When I focus on one or two things a day, my results are much more successful.

The evil one would love to keep the child of God yoked to a heavy burden, weary and confused. The yoke that Jesus would have us wear fits perfectly and allows the greatest amount of freedom. When we put our hands to the plow with Him, the work is a joy, and the harvest is one of great bounty. Will we ever learn to rest and trust in Him? Trying to feverishly build a kingdom in this fallen world will never succeed, but as we learn to rest and walk with Jesus, He leads us to a place that He has prepared for us that continues to grow in glory with each step we take. Psalms 23 is a perfect picture of the rest each believer should experience. Do you seem to be weary, and getting nowhere? I suggest you reread the 23rd Psalm. Think of yourself as one of the Gentle Shepherd's sheep, and then let Him lead you beside the still waters. Lay down when He tells you to do so, and take comfort in His strength and wisdom.

I was thinking back to different passages that speak about entering God's rest. I cannot help but think of the generation that died in the wilderness because of their unbelief. The remarkable thing is that it was the very same people who had witnessed God's miracles of deliverance. The ones that should have believed did not believe. The desert was a proving ground to God's faithfulness, and even so they just would not abandon themselves to God's care. They had been spoiled with the luxuries of Egypt in much the same way that our nation has been spoiled by prosperity. The second generation of wanderers had only known the hardships of the desert, and therefore they were receptive to even the most meager provision. The difference between the two generations was their perception of that provision. The first generation only saw the provision; the second generation was able to see the Provider. A stale crust offered by God is a treasure when the hand of provision is recognized. A feast without the presence and favor of God only fattens the flesh and hardens the heart.

I think that one of our biggest problems as believers is unbelief. Sounds like another oxymoron, doesn't it? But, think about it for a minute and you will see what I mean. I struggle with this problem a lot myself. I tend to compartmentalize my beliefs and what I trust that God will do on my behalf. Sometimes, I feel like God is in charge of some compartments, and when it comes to other compartments I feel like I have to take charge and give it my best effort. Sadly, it is in the second compartment that I see the most disappointment. Do you not feel sometimes that if something is going to happen, you have to be the one to take charge and make it happen? Perhaps when it comes to making ends meet, you believe God has a percentage of provision that he rations out and once you go over that quota it is up to you to make up the difference.

There are times that I feel like I enter battles that the Lord just will not touch. For some reason I think to myself that God must be looking at the mess I have gotten myself into, and He just sits there shaking His head in disgust saying, "You wouldn't listen. Well, you made this mess; you can clean it up now." If I were in His position I would probably be thinking and saying that very same thing. Or, could it be that He is sitting there watching me with a broken heart, because I just will not learn to trust Him in everything despite the fact that He has proven to me, time and again, that He has a provision for my every need, even the really big needs. Do you know the kind of freedom and peace we can finally have when we let go of that last, tiny percentage of control, and trust Him with every area and need in our lives? Those obstacles that we think can never be surmounted, or those deadlines that are impossible, all of those apparent impossibilities are simply opportunities for Him to show Himself strong on our behalf. Nevertheless, we push Him out of the way and say, "No thanks. I'll grit my teeth and make it through this someway or another." So, we are like the senseless horse, kicking in the "breaking stall" until we finally fall in a heap, and are willing to let Him do His miraculous work in our lives. Jesus said we are to take His yoke upon us, because His yoke is easy and His burdens are light. David the Psalmist said, "Thy gentleness has made me great." Have we been missing something, or is it possible that our ideologies and false images of God have made Him out to be some sadistic ogre who sits in the shadows, secretly enjoying our suffering? That is not the true God. That view, is a distorted view that the evil one, would probably love for us to accept.

When we strive to enter "His rest" we are not fighting to break through to some level of achievement where the spoils of battle constitute our reward for a job well done. By "striving" as it means in context, we are fighting against the tendency to try and lean on our own understanding, and our own resources: self-will, self-effort, self-promotion, to accomplish what only God can accomplish. If it is our righteousness, how good is good enough? According to God all of our righteousness amounts to nothing more than a bunch of filthy rags. When it comes to our security, it is futile to think that we can reach some level of financial or physical security that cannot be touched by outside influence. We are living in perilous times. There are no guarantees that the economy will stabilize. If the economy collapses, years of stockpiling and investing will amount to nothing but loss. We can never guarantee that our perfect health will continue even into the next week. We are all living on borrowed time. Each minute, each day, and each breath is a gift from God. The only security we have is in God alone, and the world to come. This world and the future of the world will vanish quickly. If we will make the shift, taking our eyes off the temporal, physical world and refocus on things that are eternal, we will begin to enter the rest our souls have always been searching for. When we have made the shift we will like Paul, enter a state of contentment and rest where we recognize that if we live it is all Christ, and if we die it is gain. That type of contentment can only come to the soul that has completely abandoned itself to God in absolute trust. All compartments of the inner self have been demolished and the Spirit of God inhabits that space without restriction, or measure. That is freedom. That is true rest.

Chapter Fourteen

~A Place of Refuge~

"You are my hiding place; you will protect me from trouble and
surround me with songs of deliverance."
~ Psalm 32:7

The greatest personal discovery that I found during the
North Shore project was the need for stillness before
God, not only physically, but also inwardly. We are absolutely
bombarded with a flood of noise and distractions each day.
The various forms of noise and distraction corrode our peace
and strength. But, worse yet they keep us from the place of
rest that God has provided for us in His presence.

A couple of months ago, my cousin invited me to a retreat
for men to assist with leading the worship. I was not sure at the
time if I would be able to, because my schedule was already

overloaded with ministry and work obligations. However, I felt a prompting in my spirit that this was something that the Lord wanted me to take part in. So, I packed up my guitar, some sheet music, some extra clothes, and headed off to the secluded lodge where the guys were meeting. When I arrived, I could not get my mind off all the "things" I needed to do. To make the situation worse, I was annoyed with the fact that I had so many things that needed to be done, and when I arrived they wanted me to take part in some activities that seemed really juvenile to me at the time. It all seemed really insignificant, until the guest speaker started his presentation and his text was nearly word for word what I had written in one of the chapters of my book the year before. Have you ever had that feeling where it seems like you have entered a time warp and have been transported back to an exact moment of time when God was speaking directly to your heart? He had my full attention, and I could not wait to meet with the speaker when the presentation was finished so that we could discuss our mutual findings.

The next morning the guest speaker rolled a video clip that was a compilation of all the different forms of noise we are subjected to each day. The clip only lasted about five minutes, but by the time it was finished we could actually feel the fatigue that the noise created. Nevertheless, the startling truth became evident with the next demonstration. The screen prompted us to be silent for the next five minutes, taking notice of only one sound, our breathing. Around the three-minute mark, some of the men began to squirm and look at their watches, the ceiling, the scenic views outside, the floor, or anything that would divert them from concentrating on the stillness. We could not do it. At four minutes one man jokingly, or maybe seriously shouted, "I can't stand it. I have to say something." I now understand one facet of the Scripture passage, "Do not be conformed to this world." The world cannot stand silent for any length of time, because they cannot deal with the continual voice of God speaking to them in their inner man, telling them that they are empty and lonely, sick and deprived.

People will do anything, and I do mean anything, so that they do not have to listen to that still, small voice reminding them that they have a desperate need. So, man has created countless diversions and the devil has a myriad of others that he has thrown into the mix, trying to silence God. But, you cannot silence God because, if you plug your ears, or harden your heart, He will draw your attention to the nighttime sky, the setting sun, to the miracle of birth, or to the constant ache in your heart that testifies that He is real, and you were created to live in union with Him. Men would rather stand before a crowd of noisy people than spend five minutes in silence before God. But, if we do not enter the womb of silence and contemplation, we will never find life, or our true selves. We will continue the weary existence of trying to squeeze life out of things, and experiences, apart from God. If our heart's desire is to change, then we must give God the time, the space, and our full attention. I have always been a little cautious of spiritual disciplines for the fear of falling into vain repetition and dead works, but silence in solitude is one discipline that we must perfect, or we will never have a life-changing encounter with God. He demands it, and He rewards it.

So, how do we enter this womb of silence? What does it look like? Well, obviously not everyone can take a year off and leave society behind while they seek a haven of silence in the wilderness. If you ever do get the chance, do not pass it up. It could be a divine invitation, an encounter that could change the rest of your life. Coming back to civilization was somewhat of a culture shock, but it did provide me with the opportunity to see the contrast, and what I so desperately needed to change in my life. I realized that I could not spend the rest of my days in hiding, but I could bring that hiding place into the rest of my days.

Once you have discovered true silence, it is amazing how keen your ears become to even the smallest of noises and distractions. I remember one evening while I was enjoying the silence, and expectantly listening for what God had to say, I heard what sounded like a miniature typewriter. I was about to say, "Yes, Lord I will begin typing this as soon as I get home," when the smallest little movement caught my eye-a tiny, brown mouse was chewing away on the arm of the old recliner that sat opposite the stove. He sure was a cute little guy, and he captured my attention for quite a while. He was pulling the stuffing out of the arm of the chair and chewing it up nice and soft for his little nest someplace. With a good wad of prepared sofa cushion in his mouth, he climbed down the side of the chair and disappeared behind the wood stove. I was hoping the mouse was not planning on building his nest in my clothes drawer, or guitar case. With that thought in my mind I stood up from my chair, and checked to insure that the drawers on the chest were all closed. Then, I reached for my guitar case to put it up somewhere out of reach, and thought I had better check inside the case. There were no furry inhabitants in the case, or in the guitar, but a favorite song crossed my mind. So, I took the guitar and sat down in my chair to play. As I started to sing the words, an embarrassing thought crossed my mind, and God had recaptured my attention. He allowed a scene to pass through my mind. It was a time that I had been so irritated with my wife, because God had revealed a profound truth to me and I wanted to share it with her, but the television had stolen her attention away from me. I was angry because it had taken so little to distract her from what I was trying to say. Then, the analogy hit me like only one of God's analogies can. I had been sitting in silence, inviting the God that had created the universe to come and join me for some fellowship. He was there with me in the room, and had begun to speak to me through His Word, but one of His smallest creatures had stolen the show. What kind of a friend am I? A mouse would not have captivated me if it were my brother, or someone else that had joined me for a conversation, and here I had so easily forgotten that God was with me in the room, and I was ignoring Him. This revelation has forever changed the way I view television and any other similar distraction. I wonder how often He has been trying to talk to me while I was sitting there laughing like an idiot at some television show that I would never have dared to watch with my own mother, or my pastor in the same room.

When you start making room for God in your life, you start practicing His presence. That means that you start living as if He really is with you wherever you go. The degree to which that becomes a reality is in direct proportion to the degree it affects the way you live. The more you start living as if He is in the very same room with you, the more He begins to reveal that He really is. The more you realize that He is walking with you every step of every day, the more you start clearing things out of your life that compete with His presence, or at least your perception of His presence.

Now, I immediately kill every mouse that suddenly appears. Only kidding of course, but I have stopped letting mice, or little things like them steal the opportunity that I have to connect with God, especially if I have invited Him to spend some time with me. In the same way that you must guard your house against intruders, you must find, or create space to meet with God, with the intent that you will be guarding against intruders of the mind from gaining access to your treasured time. That "space" will be your holy ground, and your place of refuge. It does not have to be a lavishly adorned study. In fact, less distractions are better, especially if your mind is prone to wander like mine is.

This may sound peculiar, but my holy ground is sometimes the bathroom. Call it the "Throne Room," if you will. Paul did some of his most inspired writing in a dungeon that shared duties with a sewer passage. It is not the location that makes it holy; it is Whom we encounter there that makes it holy. I do not consider the sound of a ventilation fan as noise. For some, that noise might be a distraction, for me it is soothing as it is sure to drown out any other competing noises, and it allows my mind to think attentively.

If light distracts you because of everything your eyes tend to explore, turn the lights out and get a little reading light so you can stay focused on the page. Simply clear your head of all your worries, the activities of today and tomorrow, and start to pray. Think about Who God is. Remember "The Lords Prayer," not to recite it over and over, but to guide you into this inner chamber where you will be meeting with God. Contemplate His majesty and omnipotence, and then contemplate your miniscule presence in contrast. Think of Psalm 138:6 –"Though the LORD is on high, he looks upon the lowly, but the proud he knows from afar." Humility is like a sweet fragrance that attracts Him. Ask for His cleansing by confessing and forsaking whatever He brings to your mind– maybe it was an attitude, or an impure thought that lingered today. Stay in this posture before Him, waiting in silence until He speaks, recalling to your mind certain events of the day, or the past, or portions of Scripture. Wait on Him, and what He has to say until you feel comfortable with expressing what is on your heart. Always allow room and >time for God to speak. I do not know how many times I have rambled on about a certain problem or some particular issue until it had turned into self-pity and I had found that I was talking to an empty room. "Me, me, me" prayers are undergirded by selfishness, which usually boils down to some form of pride trying to rise up and release a foul odor in the room. Communication is a two-way street. Some people talk, and some people hear, but that does not mean that communication has taken place.

I like to pray as I read through Scripture. As I read the Psalms it seems that certain passages are coming straight from my heart as if God is saying to me, "This is you, and I know how you feel." There is something about God's Word that is unlike any other book. When you read an emotionally touching book, it only stimulates the emotions in some form of fantasy, as you become the person in the story. Nevertheless, when you read the Word, you enter a realm where you are the story that God is writing. When we connect at that level, we experience living, life-changing, personal interaction with God.

God's Word is a treasure. Even so, many enter the Word with a sense of drudgery, hoping that God will somehow reward their duty. It is not supposed to be that way. If we are diligent to read the Word as if we were looking for buried treasure and expecting to find some, God always leaves a little "gold" here and there, but we have to value what we are looking for. When people come to the Word with the attitude that they only have a few minutes to spare it is sort of like buying a scratch-off ticket at a convenient store, hoping that it will be a winner so they can buy some gas for their car. God does not rush things, nor does He reward casual seekers. There are some things in the Kingdom that require some work, not our salvation of course, but discovering who God really is takes diligence. If we only knew all that He has to offer, we would be ashamed of our half-hearted seeking.

If someone came to us and said, "dig in this spot and you will find a treasure chest filled with diamonds and gold," we would not shovel out a few scoops and set the shovel aside. If we really believed that an enormous treasure lay below, we would dig for hours until we made the treasure our possession. It is the same with God's Word. The diamonds and gold are buried among the pages, but we must dig for them with the intensity and diligence they deserve. Once the Holy Spirit reveals the treasures, the digging becomes a joy, and we will long to enter that place of refuge each day as we find more and more of God's life-sustaining presence there. He will block the noise that has been corroding our souls, and we will sense a peace that the world cannot offer, nor take away from us.

Chapter Fifteen

~Abiding~

"Whoever dwells in the shelter of the Most High will rest in the shadow of the Almighty."
~ Psalm 91:1

*A*s I look back over the last two years I am amazed at the faithfulness of God. I was thinking about the way God led the Israelites in a roundabout way to the Promised Land. My wilderness journey stretches far beyond the last two years of my life, and where I am at the present, is not where I thought I would be a couple of years ago. Things have turned out much differently than I had planned.

My dreams and agendas have changed so many times that I have given up the idea that I am charting my own course, and God is somehow assisting me with my plans. I have found when I go off on a tangent, more often than not, it has been the result of my own scheming. A new idea will pop into my head and I will pursue it for a couple of months until it becomes painfully clear that I am like a dog that is chasing a bus; he has no idea what he will do if he catches it.

Sometimes, it feels like I am at the wheel of a big ship. I see a twinkling star on the night horizon and adjust my course to align with it, but when I do, I find the star has vanished and I am once again sailing alone in the darkness. It is in that darkness that I have discovered my weakness and ineptitude, but also the treasures that are often hidden there. The more that I realize how lost I am the more I realize that I have no business tending the elusive wheel of my life. It is in this vulnerable state of weakness that I most need to trust, but so often find myself reaching for the wheel, trying to right the ship once more.

Jesus said that apart from Him we could do nothing. I can attest to that in hindsight, but when I look at the stormy, rock-strewn waters that He seems so often to have led me through lately, impulse seems to kick in and I want to lean over His shoulder and question the coordinates. I am discovering that He wants me to step completely away from the wheel, and let Him guide the ship, even when my perceptions tell me that we are about to crash and crash hard.

So what is the secret of abiding? If "abiding" is the key to the abundant life, the life that bubbles up and becomes a torrent of living water, then how do we live in that experience? Is it something that we can generate by praying more faithfully, and diligently meditating more on the Word? I know that those of you who are reading this might not like the direction I am heading this far along in the book. Most writers have settled these antagonistic issues by now and are heading toward the tranquil waters of serene conclusions. I don't intend to write a fluffy ending to this book. I intend to write about the truth as I have experienced it. For some folks this will spark some hope; for other folks, the ones that are hoping for a shortcut on their spiritual wilderness trek, this may seem anticlimactic. The rest of this book is written for those of you who are on a soul quest, a long one at that, and desperately need a little encouragement for the rest of journey.

It has been my hope that by reading about my discoveries, you might become aware of a deep need to do whatever possible to eliminate the noise and distractions that can keep you from hearing the still, small voice of God. This book could be considered by some a case study where a man (myself) was headed in the wrong direction, had his course drastically altered, found himself in a wilderness, which seemed like a dead-end, but actually discovered that spiritual vitality could grow out of an environment of seclusion, and scarcity. At first, I thought the key was solitude, but that is the mistake that so many make. It is not the absence of people, but the absence of distraction from the single most important spiritual discipline we can ever put in to practice – **creating time, and undisturbed space to encounter God.**

As I look back over the past ten years, my greatest downfall has been the result of not giving God that creative time and space to work in my life. We are changed when we behold Him. How can we behold Him when we are always being pushed, or drawn away from His presence? This simple truth is so easy to understand, and yet so hard to put into practice. I do not know how many times I have resolved that "tomorrow, I do not care what happens; I will give God the first hour of my day." After a week I sense some progress, even notice some visual changes, but then something happens, and I begin to drift away from my commitment.

We are all stuck in the desert. After the fall of man we entered the dead zone via our family lineage under Adam. We were cursed to wander the spiritual desert of our soul, and the only things that grow readily in that type of environment are thorns and weeds. We hunger and thirst for provision that can only come from Heaven. We are all like the Israelites wandering about, still wishing for the provisions of Egypt, the things that satisfy the flesh and make us think we can squeeze some life from them. However, if God has called you out of your Egypt, the things of Egypt can never satisfy you anymore. You are in the desert and you have two choices: you can either break camp and head back the way you came, experiencing more slavery, bondage and death, or you can look to Heaven and plead for manna, and water from the Rock. You cannot take Egypt into the desert, the desert experience is meant to get you out of Egypt and Egypt out of you. So, here you are, and here am I, some where in the middle of nowhere. We need something that we cannot produce; only God can. It is received by abiding.

When I went into my time of solitude on the North Shore, I could feel that I was getting closer and closer to something that I have never experienced before with the Lord. The closer I got, the harder I searched. In fact I practically burned myself out, looking for the answer. I didn't understand what it meant to strive to enter into His rest. I thought that striving, in this sense of the word, meant I should work hard to be righteous so I could enter His presence, holy and acceptable to Him. The harder I struggled to produce my own righteousness the wearier I became. Until I stumbled across this passage in Hebrews and read it again, understanding it for the very first time.

"There remains, then, a Sabbath-rest for the people of God; for anyone who enters God's rest also rests from his own work, just as God did from his. "Let us, therefore, make every effort to enter that rest, so that no one will fall by following their example of disobedience" (Hebrews 4:9-11).

What was it that kept the Israelites out of the Promised Land? It was not the worshipping of the golden calf, or their grumbling and complaining. It was their unbelief. They didn't believe that God could care for them in the desert and lead them safely to the land He had promised them. Everything from start to finish does not come from our efforts to make things happen. It comes from recognizing our total lack of resource, our utter helplessness before God and a total abandonment with absolute trust in the goodness and mercy of God to save us.

I was reading through John Bunyan's, *The Pilgrim's Progress*, and a particular passage confirmed what I have been thinking. Pride makes us think that we can somehow force the hand of God to lift us out of our despairing condition when we have presented to Him enough tears and petitions. In the book, Christian was desperate to be delivered from his burden and he fell out of "the way," by seeking illegitimate methods of removing his burden. Then, "Evangelist," one of the book's characters, advised that he should be content to carry his burden until which time it was lifted from him. There is something utterly humbling when you know that you are carrying a burden that can only be removed by the mercy and goodwill of someone else.

We must learn to abide, and keep coming to the fount of God's presence. Has He not promised to give us everything that we need that pertains to life and godliness? Then what prevents us from entering the rest that He promises? It is our pride and insistence that He accomplish His work according to our wishes and within our time frame.

God insists that we humble ourselves before Him. Nothing humbles a person like carrying a burden of sin that all can see, but only God can lift from our shoulders. If we try to cover our sin, or decorate it in our denial, we only increase its weight and the duration we must bear it. Nevertheless, when we shoulder it, bow our heads, and walk forward into the light, humility and endurance will open the windows of grace. God will see our low estate, and draw near to us in our suffering. The Psalmist experienced this place of surrender, and abandonment to the goodness and mercy of God. David said, "But I have stilled and quieted my soul; like a weaned child with its mother, like a weaned child is my soul within me" (Psalm 131:2). Can you picture what the Psalmist is describing in the passage? Have you stilled and quieted your soul, or are you still striving to find that life-giving milk instead of trusting in God's unique provision and timing. Picture the weaned child; she has passed through a time of suffering as she has been cut off from the breast that had been the source of her sustenance and comfort. Now, the breast is hidden and the milk no longer flows, and yet she still leans her head against her mother's bosom and is content to rest, trusting her mother though the provision must now come in a different way.

I learned many things about my relationship with God from my wilderness experience. When I thought that I would encounter God in the stillness, I found that I was only starting to hear Him. It was not the destination, but only the beginning. It just goes to show that the human heart is so easily deceived. We can believe that we have moved on to the meatiest of spiritual fare, and then God reveals to us that we have not yet even found the breast.

Oh, there is so much more to learn and the closer we come to our omniscient God, the more we realize that we know very little. We must learn to hear His voice, or we will never know for sure that we are following the Good Shepherd, and not just a thief, or hireling. Look around you, and do not be quick to assume that God cannot speak through even the most trivial, mundane things of life. He is always speaking, but can we hear, or are we even listening? The very first step is to eliminate those things that obscure His whispers. In order to hear a whisper you must intensely focus. In order to hear a whisper you must lean near to the one who speaks. Only lovers and the closest of friends share secrets. Only friends take time to meet each other on a regular basis. Adam and Eve used to walk with the Lord through the garden in the cool of the evening. They drew their life from God in that special place He created for them. He still has a place that He wants to meet us, but we are always hiding among the distractions of life like Adam and Eve hid among the trees. Come near to Him, abide with Him, and do not run when you hear Him calling out, "My beloved children, where are you?" Stop striving, struggling, and analyzing things. Become like the little children in Jesus' illustrations and just draw near to Him. Abide with Him and you will be changed as you behold Him in all of His beauty and grace. Abide with Him, and you will hear the still, small voice of God saying, "this is the way walk ye in it." All the paths that He leads us upon are steadily moving us to the place of rest our hearts have always longed for and never been able to discover on our own.

Be still, and know that He is God. Be still and rest in the shadow of the Almighty.

Be still, and listen. Listen, listen, and listen some more. Listen– for the still, small voice of God.

The Challenge

*T*hank you for joining me on this project. I hope that you have discovered the same need that I discovered. We **need** God! Desperately! If we are to find Him, we must come by His terms. The best way to begin is by humbling ourselves and admitting: our need, our confusion, our waywardness, our casualness, at times our apathy, and most of all our hopelessness without Him.

If you are married, how did you get to know your spouse? Think of your best friends. How did you get to know them? All relationships take a significant amount of time. We will make time for what is truly important to us. If your spouse came to you and said, "Honey, I'm concerned about our relationship. I think we are drifting apart. You don't seem to listen to me anymore, and you never want to talk to me." Would you be concerned? Jesus said that at the end of time, "Many will say to me on that day, 'Lord, Lord, did we not prophesy in your name and in your name drive out demons and perform many miracles?' Then I will tell them plainly, 'I never knew you, away from me, you evildoers!" (Matthew 7:22, 23).

The people who said these things were actively religious people. They thought they were involved in the work of the Kingdom. They were busy doing, and concerned about many things– but they did not know Him. They did not know– "the way, the truth, and the life" (Jesus). No man can enter Heaven without knowing Jesus– not knowing "about" Jesus, but knowing Him personally, as Lord and savior. The demons know Jesus and they tremble at the mention of His name. Nevertheless, we take Him for granted everyday. I can picture Jesus as He stands at the door knocking. He waits there patiently whispering outside the door of our hearts, "Please open the door. Your eternal destiny is at stake, and I am the only one that can show you the way. But, to follow me you must hear my voice. My sheep hear my voice and they come to me when I call. I am calling you to my Word. I am calling you to prayer –come, let us reason together. I want to make you a new creation, but your priorities will not allow. What shall it profit you if you gain the whole world, but lose your own soul?"

Here is the challenge: Tithe your time. You have 24 hours of it each day. A tenth of that is 2.4 hours. 2.4 hours of your undivided attention before God each day will change your life, and possibly, your destiny. 2.4 hours is roughly 144 minutes. How often do you eat each day to sustain your mortal body– three times, or maybe four? Breakfast is the most important meal; treat your spiritual food with the same importance. Eat a heavy meal in the morning. Light snacks in the in between times, keep the body and soul functioning at optimum performance. Never skip meals. I challenge you to give God no less than 144 minutes a day. Take note of what happens over the next few weeks and months. Keep a journal, and record the ways God reveals Himself to you. Divide those 144 minutes with the bulk at the beginning of the day, and guard those time slots as sacred. Honor God by putting Him first in your time, and He will reward your commitment to seek Him.

Put your priorities in writing somewhere that you will see them everyday. If you want to be a friend of God, you must treat Him like a friend. If you told Him that you would meet with Him at 7a.m. then you should be on time, just like you would if you were meeting any other friend. Our actions reveal our hearts motives, and God does not go where He is not truly wanted.

Pray that God will give you an insatiable desire to know Him. God answered this prayer with me by hiding His face from me for a season. I felt like I had been abandoned, but it only strengthened my desire to know Him and seek Him more. Hunger is a good thing if God creates it. If God creates the hunger, He intends to satisfy it. Read the Word even when you do not want to. You may think that there was no impact from a certain passage, but God promises that His Word does not return to Him void. You may not remember what you read last week, but God is able to bless your reading regardless. Sometimes, I do not remember what I had for breakfast, but I do know that it gave me strength for the day.

Keep an expectant heart before God. Keep your eyes and ears open, He can speak through the most trivial, unexpected things like; donkeys, burning bushes, storms, sorrow, joy, and yes, even miracles. Take note of how God speaks to you.

He often speaks to me most clearly through nature. For you it might be children, spouses, or circumstances. Never limit God, and He will show you amazing things.

Find out the greatest source of noise in your life. It could be your hobbies. It could be a habit. It could be the television. It could be good things, even church related activities. It could be anything that keeps you from meeting with God, or walking with Him throughout the day. It will distract you and capture your thoughts even when you are sitting before God in prayer. It could be your family. Explain your commitment to them. They may not understand why you are suddenly disappearing for an hour and locking the study door behind you. It could be the phone. If it is the phone, remember "Who" should receive the greatest priority, and everyone else gets the remaining 22.6 hours of the day. Don't shortchange the Lord. There is no one more deserving of your time and total attention.

Finally, stick with the commitment until it becomes a natural habit. Eat three square meals of the Word daily, and treat prayer like breathing. As much as you possibly can, engage in a dialogue with the Lord through out the day, and you will soon discover that you are walking naturally with the Lord every hour of the day. Get the noise out of His way, and you will begin to hear even His smallest whispers when you treasure every word He has to say. Be still, and you will know that He is God. It is a battle, but if you will indeed battle for that time, space, and stillness, you will discover the eternal rewards and mysteries God has in store for you.

Acknowledgments

To the Lord Jesus Christ, thank you for lifting another beggar out of the dung hill, and showing me the path to abundant life, that eternal life, found only in you. Thank you for opening doors that no man can shut, and closing doors that I have tried so hard to open. Your timing is always best. Thank you for your wisdom, and making all things new.

To my loving wife Rachelle, thank you for walking with me on such a long journey. Thank you for being my best friend, my partner, my lover, and companion for life. You have proven faithful and true, come what may. I pray that every dream God has for you will come true, and be so much bigger than you can possibly imagine.

Thanks for all of your suggestions, and your eye for beauty. Your photography has captured the scenic appeal I had intended for this book.

To Dr. Charles Shepson, a dear friend of the family, a respected pillar in the Christian and Missionary Alliance community, and a worthy role model for budding writers like me. Thank you for all of your hard work on this project. Yours is a special gift. I thank you for encouraging me to become a better writer, while preserving my tender self-esteem. Thank you for the many years you have blessed our family as well as the rest of the family of God. It was an honor to work on this project together and I pray there will be more.

To my family, I love you all. If I were to thank all of you individually another volume would be required. I am grateful for your many prayers over the years, believing that one day God would do the miraculous in my life. He has, and He continues to do so. In regards to your anonymous support, friendship, and much needed encouragement, I will be forever grateful. In the measure you have reached out to me, the least, you have reached out to our Lord, and great will be your reward.

To Mom and Dad, you have run your race well. Thank you for instilling in each of us a hope that has proved to be an anchor in some of life's greatest storms.

To the dedicated professionals at Westbow Press, thanks for helping me launch a dream. You are unbelievably patient, and I wish you the best with all of your future endeavors. I pray our relationships will continue with many more projects to come.

24372892R00086

Printed in Great Britain
by Amazon